DEBBIE MUMM'S®
HOME COMINGS

Dear Friends,

One of the most satisfying things in life is gathering family and friends for a holiday or special occasion celebration. Those events when people come together from far and near are the most memorable and joyous of occasions. Preparing for these events is a big part of the fun and this book is loaded with projects and ideas for setting the scene for joy-filled reunions and homecomings.

Whenever family gathers together for a springtime celebration, your get-together will be enhanced by a beautiful basket quilt on the wall or a bright burst of color on the sofa. Rally friends and family for a 4th of July barbecue festooned with red, white, and blue banners and pillows. Haunt them at Halloween with patchwork quilts, spooky pillows, and timely table runners.

Bring the rich colors and traditions of Autumn to your home with wall and lap quilts, table quilts, and even a scarecrow. Make Christmas the merriest with birds, banners, and a log cabin legacy quilt.

Revel in each season, each celebration! I hope that this book inspires years of sewing fun as you create quilts and crafts that are sure to become an important part of each homecoming celebration.

Celebrate all year long!
Debbie Mumm

©2009 by Debbie Mumm • Leisure Arts, Inc., 5701 Ranch Drive, Little Rock, AR 72223 • www.leisurearts.com

Springtime SAMPLER

Independence Day CELEBRATIONS

Halloween HAPPENINGS

Harvest CELEBRATIONS

Holiday TRADITIONS

Springtime
SAMPLER

Family GATHERINGS

Gather family and friends for a springtime celebration of fun, food, and fanciful décor. Sunshiny colors, fantastic flowers, and Earth Day exuberance will make your spring festivities, events to remember.

Blossom Basket Wall Quilt

Scattered Flowers Lap Quilt

Four Flower Pillow

Flower Basket Pillow

Spring Flowers Door Banner

Earth Day Wall Quilt

Earth Day Tea Towels

Earth Day Table Topper

Blossom Basket
WALL QUILT

Blossom Basket Wall Quilt Finished Size: 27" x 27"	FIRST CUT		SECOND CUT	
	Number of Strips or Pieces	Dimensions	Number of Pieces	Dimensions
Fabric A Top Background ⅓ yard	1	8½" x 42"	1	8½" x 20½"
Fabric B Bottom Background ½ yard	1	12½" x 42"	2	12½" x 10½"
Fabric C Basket-Light ⅙ yard	1	4½" x 42"	2	4½" squares
Fabric D Basket-Medium/Light ⅓ yard	1	8½" x 42"	2 2	8½" squares 2½" squares
Fabric E Basket-Medium ⅜ yard	1	10½" x 42"	2 2 2	10½" squares 6½" squares 2½" squares
Fabric F Basket-Dark ⅙ yard	1	4½" x 42"	2	4½" squares
First Border ¼ yard	4	1½" x 42"	2 2	1½" x 22½" 1½" x 20½"
Outside Border ⅓ yard	4	2½" x 42"	2 2	2½" x 26½" 2½" x 22½"
Binding ⅜ yard	4	2¾" x 42"		
Backing - ⅞ yard Batting - 31" x 31" Flower & Leaf Appliqués - Assorted scraps Lightweight Fusible Web - ⅓ yard				

Fabric Requirements and Cutting Instructions

Read all instructions before beginning and use ¼"-wide seam allowances throughout. Read Cutting Strips and Pieces on page 92 prior to cutting fabric.

Getting Started

Showcase the first flowers of spring by making this charming wall quilt. Refer to Accurate Seam Allowance on page 92. Whenever possible use Assembly Line Method on page 92. Press seams in direction of arrows.

Making the Quilt

1. Refer to Quick Corner Triangles on page 92. Making quick corner triangle units, sew one 4½" Fabric F square and one 2½" Fabric D square to one 12½" x 10½" Fabric B piece as shown. Press.

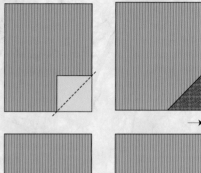

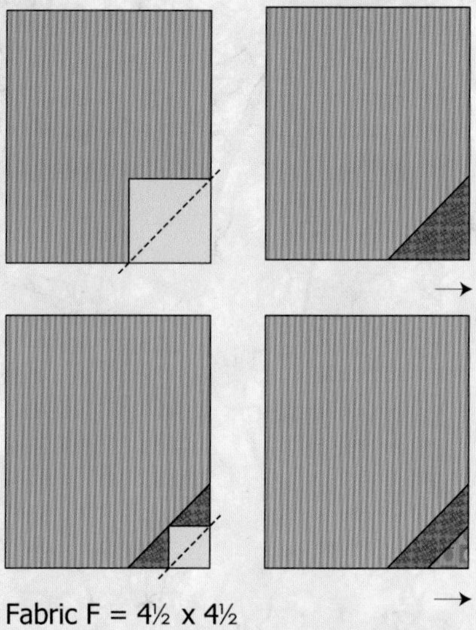

Fabric F = 4½ x 4½
Fabric D = 2½ x 2½
Fabric B = 12½ x 10½

2. Repeat step 1 to sew one 4½" Fabric F square and one 2½" Fabric D square to one 12½" x 10½" Fabric B piece, checking orientation of angle prior to sewing. Press.

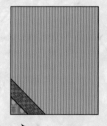

Celebrate the first signs of spring with this joyful basket of fabric flowers. Quick Corner Triangles make the basket quick and easy and the fanciful flowers will add color and whimsy to all your springtime gatherings.

3. Making a quick corner triangle unit, sew one 10½" Fabric E square to each unit from step 1 and step 2 as shown. Press. Make two, one of each variation.

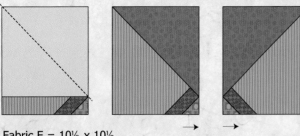

Fabric E = 10½ x 10½
Units from step 1 and 2

4. Making a quick corner triangle unit, sew one 8½" Fabric D square to each unit from step 3. Press. Make two, one of each variation.

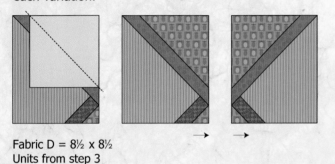

Fabric D = 8½ x 8½
Units from step 3

5. Making a quick corner triangle unit, sew one 6½" Fabric E square to each unit from step 4. Press. Make two, one of each variation.

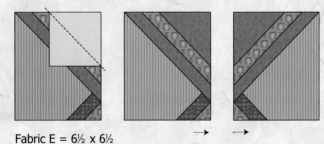

Fabric E = 6½ x 6½
Units from step 4

6. Making a quick corner triangle unit, sew one 4½" Fabric C square to each unit from step 5. Press. Make two, one of each variation.

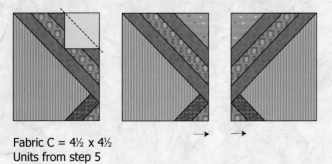

Fabric C = 4½ x 4½
Units from step 5

7. Making a quick corner triangle unit, sew one 2½" Fabric E square to one unit from step 6. Press. Make two, one of each variation.

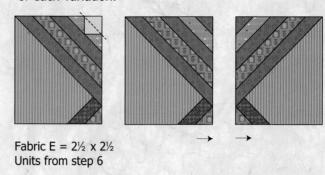

Fabric E = 2½ x 2½
Units from step 6

8. Referring to photo on page 7, sew units from step 7 together. Press. Sew this unit to 8½" x 20½" Fabric A piece. Press seam toward Fabric A.

9. Sew unit from step 8 between two 1½" x 20½" First Border strips. Press seams toward border. Sew this unit between two 1½" x 22½" First Border strips. Press.

10. Sew unit from step 9 between two 2½" x 22½" Outside Border strips. Press seams toward Outside border. Sew this unit between two 2½" x 26½" Outside Border strips. Press.

Adding the Appliqués

Refer to appliqué instructions on page 93. Our instructions are for Quick-Fuse Appliqué, but if you prefer hand appliqué, reverse templates and add ¼"-wide seam allowances.

1. Use patterns on pages 8, 9, and 15 to trace Flowers (one #1, two #2, two #3, one #4, two #5, and one #6), and two leaves on paper side of fusible web. Use appropriate fabrics to prepare all appliqués for fusing.

2. Refer to photo on page 7 to position and fuse appliqués to quilt. Finish appliqué edges with machine satin stitch or other decorative stitching as desired.

Layering and Finishing

1. Referring to Layering the Quilt on page 94, arrange and baste backing, batting, and top together. Hand or machine quilt as desired.

2. Refer to Binding the Quilt on page 94. Using 2¾"-wide binding strips, bind quilt to finish.

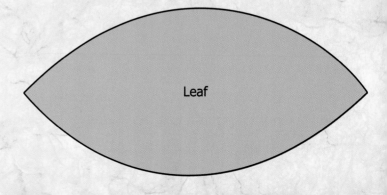

Leaf

Tracing Line _____

Flower #5

Flower #4

Flower #2

Flower #1

Flower #3

Scattered Flowers
LAP QUILT

Scattered Flowers Lap Quilt Finished Size: 48" x 62"	FIRST CUT		SECOND CUT	
	Number of Strips or Pieces	Dimensions	Number of Pieces	Dimensions
Fabric A Yellow ⅓ yard	1 1	6½" x 42" 4½" x 42"	6 6	6½" squares 4½" squares
Fabric B Light Green ½ yard	1 1	8½" x 42" 6½" x 42"	6 6	8½" x 4½" 6½" squares
Fabric C Medium Green ⅓ yard	1 1	6½" x 42" 4½" x 42"	6 6	6½" squares 4½" squares
Fabric D Blue/Green ½ yard	1 3	8½" x 42" 2½" x 42"	6 6	8½" x 4½" 2½" x 14½"
Fabric E Medium/Light Blue ⅓ yard	1 1	6½" x 42" 4½" x 42"	6 6	6½" squares 4½" squares
Fabric F Medium Blue ½ yard	1 1	8½" x 42" 4½" x 42"	6 6	8½" x 4½" 4½" squares
Fabric G Dark Blue ½ yard	1 3	8½" x 42" 2½" x 42"	6 6	8½" x 4½" 2½" x 14½"
First Border ¼ yard	5	1" x 42"		
Outside Border ½ yard	6	2½" x 42"		
Binding ⅝ yard	6	2¾" x 42"		
Backing - 3 yards Batting - 54" x 68" Flower Appliqués - Assorted scraps Lightweight Fusible Web - ⅔ yard				

Fabric Requirements and Cutting Instructions

Read all instructions before beginning and use ¼"-wide seam allowances throughout. Read Cutting Strips and Pieces on page 92 prior to cutting fabric.

Getting Started

This quilt uses only squares and rectangles making it easy to construct, plus an additional touch of fun has been added with these simple appliquéd flowers. Blocks measure 14½" square (unfinished). Refer to Accurate Seam Allowance on page 92. Whenever possible use Assembly Line Method on page 92. Press seams in direction of arrows.

Making the Blocks

1. Sew one 4½" Fabric A square and one 4½" Fabric F square together. Press seam toward Fabric F. Sew this unit to one 8½" x 4½" Fabric D piece as shown. Press. Make six.

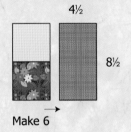

Make 6

2. Sew one unit from step 1 to one 8½" x 4½" Fabric B piece as shown. Press. Make six.

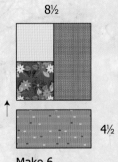

Make 6

Who needs April showers when you can grow a colorful garden of spring flowers at your sewing machine! Flower appliqués are scattered randomly on this easy-to-piece lap quilt, making it a perfect way to add bright color and texture to your springtime home.

3. Sew one 6½" Fabric C square to one 6½" Fabric E square. Press seam toward Fabric E. Sew this unit to unit from step 2 as shown. Press. Make six.

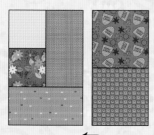

Make 6

4. Sew one 2½" x 14½" Fabric G strip to one unit from step 3 as shown. Press. Make six and label Block 1. Block measures 14½" square.

Block 1

14½

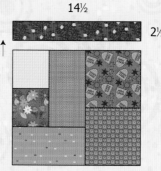

2½

Make 6
Block measures 14½" square

5. Repeat steps 1-4 to make six of Block 2. Step 1 uses Fabrics C, E, and G; step 2, Fabric F; step 3, Fabrics A and B; and step 4, Fabric D. Block measures 14½" square.

Block 2

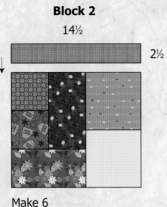

Make 6
Block measures 14½" square

Adding the Appliqués

Refer to appliqué instructions on page 93. Our instructions are for Quick-Fuse Appliqué, but if you prefer hand appliqué, add ¼"-wide seam allowances.

1. Use patterns on page 9 to trace Flowers (Four #2, four #3, two #4, and seven #5) on paper side of fusible web. Use appropriate fabrics to prepare all appliqués for fusing.

2. Refer to photo on page 11 and layout to position and fuse appliqués to Blocks 1 and 2. Finish appliqué edges with machine satin stitch or other decorative stitching as desired.

Assembling the Quilt

Referring to photo on page 11 and layout, arrange and sew together four rows of three blocks each, alternating Block 1 and Block 2 placement. Check orientation of blocks before assembly. Repress block seams if necessary. Press seams in opposite direction from row to row.

Adding the Borders

1. Refer to Adding the Borders on page 94. Sew 1" x 42" First Border strips together end-to-end to make one continuous 1"-wide First Border strip. Measure quilt through center from side to side. Cut two 1"-wide First Border strips to this measurement. Sew to top and bottom of quilt. Press seams toward border.

2. Measure quilt through center from top to bottom including border just added. Cut two 1"-wide First Border strips to this measurement. Sew to sides of quilt. Press.

3. Refer to steps 1 and 2 to join, measure, trim, and sew 2½"-wide Outside Border strips to top, bottom, and sides of quilt. Press.

Layering and Finishing

1. Cut backing crosswise into two equal pieces. Sew pieces together lengthwise to make one 54" x 80" (approximate) backing piece. Press and trim to 54" x 68".

2. Referring to Layering the Quilt on page 94, arrange and baste backing, batting, and top together. Hand or machine quilt as desired.

3. Refer to Binding the Quilt on page 94. Sew 2¾" x 42" binding strips end-to-end to make one continuous 2¾"-wide binding strip. Bind quilt to finish.

Scattered Flowers Lap Quilt Finished Size: 48" x 62"

PILLOWS

Toss a pillow on a chair for instant springtime!

Making the Four Flower Pillow

Refer to appliqué instructions on page 93. Our instructions are for Quick-Fuse Appliqué, but if you prefer hand appliqué, add ¼"-wide seam allowances.

1. Sew one 6½" Background square between two 1" x 6½" Accent Border pieces. Press seams toward border. Sew this unit between two 1" x 7½" Accent Border pieces. Press.

2. Sew unit from step 1 between two 2½" x 7½" Outside Border pieces. Press seams toward border. Sew this unit between two 2½" x 11½" Outside Border pieces. Press.

3. Use patterns on page 9 to trace four #3 flowers on paper side of fusible web. Use appropriate fabrics to prepare all appliqués for fusing. Refer to photo to position and fuse appliqués to unit from step 2. Finish appliqué edges with machine satin stitch or other decorative stitching as desired.

4. Refer to Finishing Pillows on page 94, step 1, to prepare pillow top for quilting. Quilt as desired.

5. Use two 8½" x 11½" backing pieces and refer to Finishing Pillows, page 95, steps 2-4, to sew backing.

6. Insert 11" pillow form or refer to Pillow Forms page 95 to make a pillow form if desired.

Making the Flower Basket Pillow

Refer to Quick-Fuse Appliqué instructions on page 93.

1. Sew one 8½" Background square between two 3½" x 8½" Border strips. Press seams toward border. Sew this unit between two 3½" x 14½" Border strips. Press.

2. Use patterns on page 15 to trace #6 flower, basket, and two flower basket leaves on paper side of fusible web. Use appropriate fabrics to prepare all appliqués for fusing. Refer to photo to position and fuse appliqués to unit from step 1. Finish appliqué edges with machine satin stitch or other decorative stitching as desired.

3. Refer to Finishing Pillows on page 94, step 1, to prepare pillow top for quilting. Quilt as desired.

4. Use two 10" x 14½" backing pieces and refer to Finishing Pillows, page 94, steps 2-4, to sew backing.

5. Insert 14" pillow form or refer to Pillow Forms on page 95 to make a pillow form if desired.

Materials Needed
Finished Size: 11" x 11"

Background - ¼ yard
   One - 6½" square
Accent Border - ⅛ yard
   Two - 1" x 7½"
   Two - 1" x 6½"
Outside Border - ⅛ yard
   Two - 2½" x 11½"
   Two - 2½" x 7½"
Backing - ⅛ yard
   Two - 8½" x 11½"
Lining and Batting - 13" x 13"
Appliqué Flowers - Assorted scraps
Lightweight Fusible Web - ⅛ yard
11" Pillow Form
   OR ⅜ yard Muslin & Polyester Fiberfill

Materials Needed
Finished Size: 14" x 14"

Background - ⅓ yard
   One - 8½" square
Border - ¼ yard
   Two - 3½" x 14½"
   Two - 3½" x 8½"
Backing - ⅓ yard
   Two - 10" x 14½"
Lining and Batting - 16" x 16"
Appliqués - Assorted scraps
Lightweight Fusible Web - ¼ yard
14" Pillow Form
   OR ½ yard Muslin & Polyester Fiberfill

Spring Flowers
DOOR BANNER

Flowers are a sure sign of spring. Luxurious wool in springtime hues makes this banner a fun hand-sewing project.

See Materials List on next page.

Making the Banner

Refer to appliqué instructions on page 93. Our instructions are for Quick-Fuse Appliqué, but if you prefer hand appliqué, use cotton fabric, reverse templates and add ¼"-wide seam allowances.

1. Use patterns on page 15 to trace one #6 flower and three #7 flowers, basket and two flower basket leaves on paper side of fusible web. Use appropriate fabrics to prepare all appliqués for fusing.

2. Iron 12½" lightweight fusible web square to the back of 13" Fabric B square. From this piece, cut one 8½" x 9" piece, and three 2½" squares. Refer to diagram to position and fuse Fabric B pieces to 12" x 15¾" Fabric A piece.

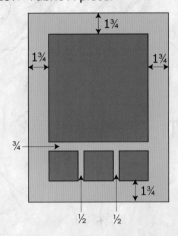

3. Refer to photo to position and fuse basket, flowers, and leaves to unit from step 2.

4. Option: Our banner uses hand blanket stitch, but machine blanket stitch can be used if desired. Refer to Embroidery Guide on page 94 for a blanket stitch. Using a blanket stitch and embroidery floss or Perle cotton, stitch around all squares and rectangles, large flower and leaves. Do not add stitching to Fabric A outside edge or the small flowers. Note: We used two shades of green floss for Fabric B and leaf pieces, blue floss on large flower, and orange floss on basket.

5. For each small flower use yellow floss and a straight stitch to add a circle to center of flower approximately ¼" away from center appliqué.

6. Center completed unit over 13" x 17" Fabric B piece. Pin in place. Use blue floss to stitch layers together with hand or machine blanket stitch.

7. Trim Fabric B backing piece ¼" away from Fabric A outside edge. Hang or displayed as desired.

Materials Needed

All Fabrics are Wool or Felted Wool*

Fabric A (Background) - ⅜ yard
    One - 12" x 15¾"

Fabric B (Appliqué Background and Backing) - ½ yard
    One - 13" x 17"
    One - 13" square
    Three - 2½" square

Appliqués - Assorted scraps

Lightweight Fusible Web - 1 yard

Embroidery Floss/Perle Cotton (Optional)
    Blue, Yellow, Orange, and Green (two shades)

*See Tips for Felting Wool on page 95.

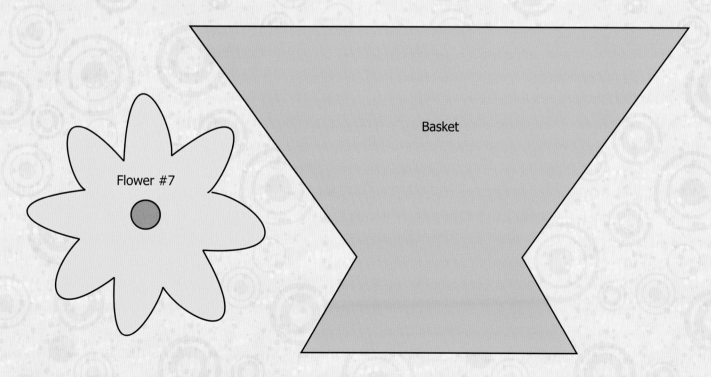

Flower #6

Flower Basket Leaf

Tracing Line_____

Flower #7

Basket

Earth Day
WALL QUILT

Earth Day Quilt Finished Size: 32" x 31"	FIRST CUT	
	Number of Strips or Pieces	Dimensions
Fabric A Appliqué Background ⅓ yard each of 2 Fabrics	3*	9½" x 10½" *cut for each fabric
Fabric B Strip Set Blocks ⅛ yard each of 4 Fabrics	1*	1¼" x 42" *cut for each fabric
Fabric C Strip Set Blocks ⅛ yard each of 4 Fabrics	2*	1¼" x 42" *cut for each fabric
First Border ⅙ yard	4	1" x 27½"
Outside Border ⅓ yard	2 2	2" x 30½" 2" x 28½"
Binding ⅜ yard	4	2¾" x 42"
Backing - 1 yard Batting - 36" x 35" Tree Trunk Appliqués - ¼ yard each of 3 Fabrics Leaf Appliqués - ⅛ yard each of 3 Fabrics Lightweight Fusible Web - 1 yard		

Fabric Requirements and Cutting Instructions

Read all instructions before beginning and use ¼"-wide seam allowances throughout. Read Cutting Strips and Pieces on page 92 prior to cutting fabric.

Getting Started

This simple, yet graphic quilt depicts the early foliage of spring trees. Each Appliquéd Block measures 9½" x 10½" (unfinished). Strip Set Blocks measure 3½" square (unfinished). Refer to Accurate Seam Allowance on page 92. Whenever possible use Assembly Line Method on page 92. Press seams in direction of arrows.

Making the Appliqué Blocks

Refer to appliqué instructions on page 93. Our instructions are for Quick-Fuse Appliqué, but if you prefer hand appliqué, reverse templates and add ¼"-wide seam allowances.

1. Use patterns on page 18 to trace six trees on paper side of fusible web. Use appropriate fabrics to prepare all appliqués for fusing.

2. Refer to photo on page 17 to position and fuse appliqués to 9½" x 10½" Fabric A pieces. Finish appliqué edges with machine satin stitch or other decorative stitching as desired. Make six.

Making the Strip Set Blocks

1. Sew together lengthwise four 1¼" x 42" assorted Fabric B and C strips to make a strip set as shown. Press. Cut strip set into six 3½"-wide segments as shown.

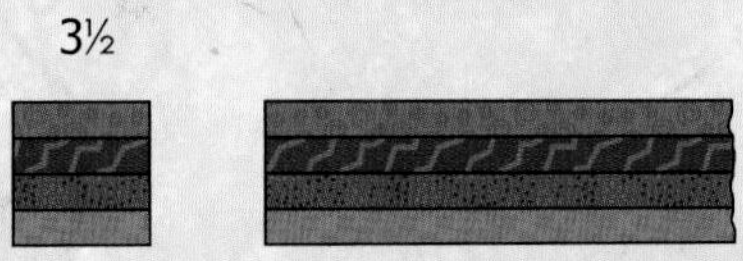

3½

Cut 6 segments

2. Repeat step 1 to make two strip sets units using assorted Fabric B and C strips. Cut each strip set into six 3½"-wide segments.

3½   3½

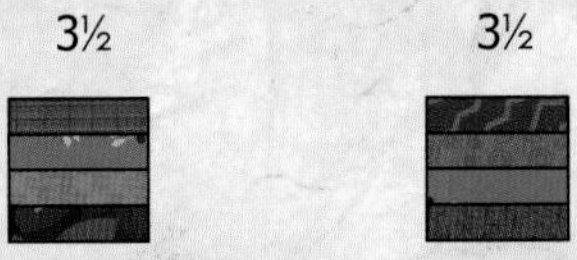

Cut 6 segments   Cut 6 segments

3. Referring to photo on page 17, arrange and sew together three Strip Set Blocks, one of each variation as shown, to make a Strip Set Row. Check orientation of blocks prior to sewing. Press. Make six.

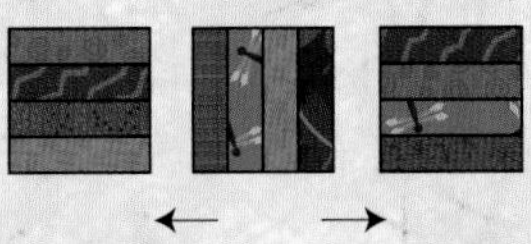

← →

Make 6
(Refer to photo to arrange segments.)

Go green and celebrate our wonderful earth by making this quick quilt from your fabric stash or scraps. The simplicity of the appliqué symbolizes the message "reduce, reuse, recycle."

Assembling the Quilt

This quilt uses vertical row construction.

1. Referring to photo, arrange and sew together two Appliqué Blocks and two Strip Set rows. Press. Make three.

2. Referring to photo, arrange and sew rows together. Press.

Adding the Borders

1. Sew two 1" x 27½" First Border strips to top and bottom of quilt. Press toward borders. Sew two 1" x 27½" First Border strips to sides of quilt. Press.

2. Sew two 2" x 28½" Outside Border strips to top and bottom of quilt. Press toward borders. Sew two 2" x 30½" Outside Border strips to sides of quilt. Press.

Layering and Finishing

1. Referring to Layering the Quilt on page 94, arrange and baste backing, batting, and top together. Hand or machine quilt as desired.

2. Refer to Binding the Quilt on page 94. Using 2¾"-wide binding strips, bind quilt to finish.

Medium Leaf

Small Leaf

Earth Day Tea Towels

Earth Day Quilt
Patterns are reversed for use with
Quick-Fuse Appliqué (page 93)

Tracing Line _____
Tracing Line ....
(will be hidden behind other fabrics)

Earth Day
TEA TOWELS

Decorate your kitchen or bath with nature-loving cotton towels embellished with leaf appliqués. Accent the towels with a table topper made from left-over strip set blocks from the wall quilt.

Earth Day Tea Towels
Finished Size: 15" x 25" Finished Size: 13" x 21"

Earth Day Table Topper
Finished Size: 14" x 14"

Making the Appliquéd Towels

Refer to appliqué instructions on page 93. Our instructions are for Quick-Fuse Appliqué, but if you prefer hand appliqué, reverse templates and add ¼"-wide seam allowances.

1. Fold ¼" to the wrong side of 2½" x 22" Appliqué Background strip along both 22" sides. Press.

2. Measure and mark 1½" from one end of 14" x 22" Appliquéd Towel piece. Align folded strip from step 1 along this mark. Top stitch in place.

3. Use patterns on page 18 to trace three small leaves on paper side of fusible web. Use appropriate fabrics to prepare all appliqués for fusing.

4. Fold towel in thirds lengthwise, press, then unfold. This will be used as a guide for centering appliqués. Refer to photo to position appliqués on towel strip in center section only. Finish appliqué edges with machine satin stitch or other decorative stitching as desired. [For towel with one leaf, omit fabric strip. Trace one 3" square and one medium leaf appliqué on paper side of fusible web. Prepare fabrics for fusing. Refer to photo to center, fuse, and stitch appliqués to towel.]

5. Fold all sides of towel piece ¼" to the wrong side and press. Fold edges under another ¼", press, and top stitch in place.

Making the Background Towels

Fold all sides of Large Towel fabric piece ¼" to the wrong side and press. Fold all edges under another ¼", press, and top stitch in place. Display towels as desired. Our towels were all folded in thirds lengthwise, placing one large towel under each small towel.

Materials Needed
For Two Appliquéd Towels

Appliquéd Towels
  ½ yard each of two complementary fabrics
  Two - 14" x 22" pieces

Appliqué Background - ⅛ yard
  One - 2½" x 22" strip

Appliqués - Assorted scraps

Lightweight Fusible Web - ⅛ yard

Background Towels
  ½ yard each of two complementary fabrics
  Two - 16" x 26" pieces

Earth Day Table Topper

Cut a total of sixteen 3½"-wide segments from left-over Earth Day Wall Quilt (page 16) strip sets. If unable to cut appropriate number of Strip Set Blocks then cut and sew 1¼" x 3½" assorted Fabric B and C pieces to make additional 3½"-wide blocks. Sew four blocks together alternating direction of segments. Make two. Sew four blocks together reversing directions from previous row. Make two. Sew rows together, alternating rows. Sew 1½"-wide border strips to all sides and finish as desired.

Independence Day CELEBRATIONS

Summertime REUNIONS

Family and friends gather in the back yard for a good old-fashioned 4th of July celebration filled with festive patriotic décor, picnic fare, fireworks, and flags.

Liberty Lap Quilt

Sand Candles

Americana Wall Quilt

Nine-Patch Pillow

Lone Star Pillows

Americana Door Banner

Patriotic Flowerpot

Star Spangled Pillow

Liberty
LAP QUILT

Liberty Lap Quilt Finished Size: 53" x 67"	FIRST CUT		SECOND CUT	
	Number of Strips or Pieces	Dimensions	Number of Pieces	Dimensions
Fabric A Block Background ⅞ yard each of 2 Fabrics	2* 10*	4" x 42" 2" x 42" *cut for each fabric	12* 192*	4" squares 2" squares
Fabric B Center & Corner Triangles ½ yard each of 2 Fabrics	1* 2*	7" x 42" 4" x 42" *cut for each fabric	3* 12*	7" squares 4" squares
Fabric C Center, Flying Geese & Block Border 1¼ yards each of 2 Fabrics	1* 9* 10*	7" x 42" 2" x 42" 1½" x 42" *cut for each fabric	3* 96* 12* 12*	7" squares 2" x 3½" 1½" x 14½" 1½" x 12½"
First Border ⅓ yard	6	1½" x 42"		
Second Border ⅓ yard	6	1½" x 42"		
Outside Border ⅔ yard OR 1⅞ yards (Directional)	6 4	3½" x 42" (Non -Directional) OR 3½" x Length of Fabric (Stripe runs parallel to selvage)		
Binding ⅝ yard	7	2¾" x 42"		
Backing - 3½ yards Batting - 61" x 75"				

Fabric Requirements and Cutting Instructions

Read all instructions before beginning and use ¼"-wide seam allowances throughout. Read Cutting Strips and Pieces on page 92 prior to cutting fabric.

Getting Started

Display your patriotic spirit all summer with this classy quilt or use it as a great addition to a nautical-themed room with its traditional red, white, and blue color combination. Blocks measure 14½" square (unfinished). Refer to Accurate Seam Allowance on page 92. Whenever possible use Assembly Line Method on page 92. Press seams in direction of arrows.

Making the Blocks

1. Refer to Quick Corner Triangles on page 92. Making quick corner triangle units, sew two 2" Fabric A squares to one 2" x 3½" Fabric C piece as shown. Press. Make ninety-six.

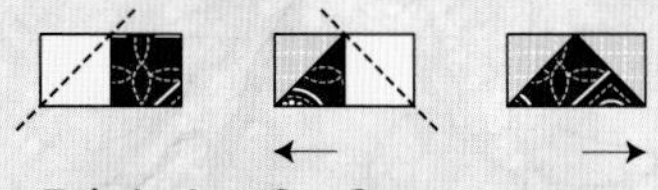

Fabric A = 2 x 2
Fabric C = 2 x 3½
Make 96

2. Sew four units from step 1 together as shown. Press. Make twenty-four.

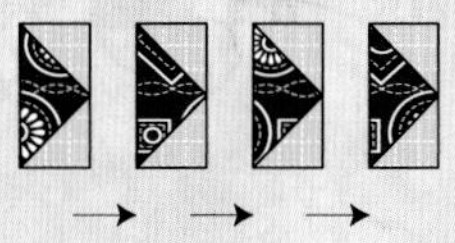

Make 24

3. Draw a diagonal line on wrong side of one 4" Fabric A square. Place marked square and one 4" Fabric B square right sides together. Sew scant ¼" away from drawn line on both sides to make half-square triangles as shown. Make twelve. Cut on drawn line and press. Square to 3½". This will make twenty-four half-square triangle units.

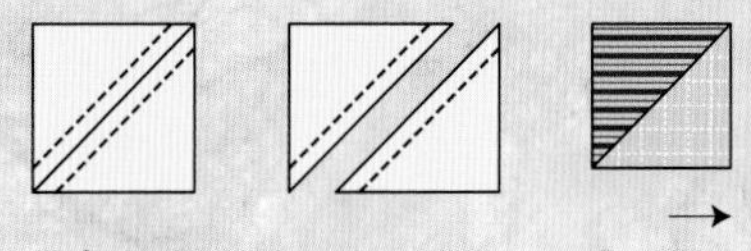

Fabric A = 4 x 4
Fabric B = 4 x 4
Make 12

Square to 3½
Make 24
Half-square Triangles

4. Sew one unit from step 2 between two units from step 3 as shown, checking orientation of step 3 units prior to sewing. Press. Make twelve.

Make 12

Curl up under the stars for the fireworks finale wrapped in this patriotic pleaser. Red, white, and blue blocks stylishly convey a message of patriotism and evoke the simple pleasures of life in this country that we love.

5. Draw a diagonal line on wrong side of one 7" Fabric B square. Place marked square and one 7" Fabric C square right sides together. Sew scant ¼" away from drawn line on both sides to make half-square triangles as shown. Make three. Cut on drawn line and press. Square to 6½". This will make six half-square triangle units.

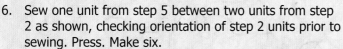

Fabric B = 7 x 7
Fabric C = 7 x 7
Make 3

← Square to 6½
Make 6
Half-square Triangles

6. Sew one unit from step 5 between two units from step 2 as shown, checking orientation of step 2 units prior to sewing. Press. Make six.

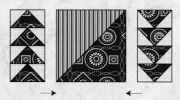

Make 6

7. Sew one unit from step 6 between two units from step 4 as shown. Press. Make six.

Make 6

8. Sew one unit from step 7 between two 1½" x 12½" Fabric C strips. Press. Sew this unit between two 1½" x 14½" Fabric C strips as shown. Press and label Block 1. Make six. Block measures 14½" square.

1½" **Block 1** 1½"

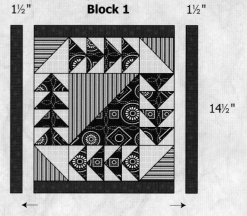

14½"

Make 6
Block measures 14½" square

Liberty Lap Quilt Finished Size: 53" x 67"

9. Referring to steps 1-8 and using remaining Fabric A, B, and C pieces, make six of Block 2 as shown, checking orientation of center unit prior to sewing. Block measures 14½" square.

1½" **Block 2** 1½"

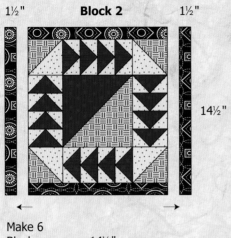

14½"

Make 6
Block measures 14½" square

10. Refer to photo on page 23 and layout on page 24 for steps 10-12. Sew one Block 2 between two of Block 1. Press toward Block 2. Make two.

11. Sew one Block 1 between two of Block 2. Press toward Block 2. Make two.

12. Sew rows from step 10 and 11 together alternating row placement. Press.

Adding the Borders

1. Refer to Adding the Borders on page 94. Sew 1½" x 42" First Border strips together end-to-end to make one continuous 1½"-wide First Border strip. Measure quilt through center from side to side. Cut two 1½"-wide First Border strips to this measurement. Sew to top and bottom of quilt. Press seams toward border.

2. Measure quilt through center from top to bottom including border just added. Cut two 1½"-wide First Border strips to this measurement. Sew to sides of quilt. Press.

3. Refer to steps 1 and 2 to join, measure, trim, and sew 1½"-wide Second Border, and 3½"-wide Outside Border strips to top, bottom, and sides of quilt. Press. Note: If using directional fabric the Outside borders will not need to be pieced, side borders are added first and top and bottom borders last.

Layering and Finishing

1. Cut backing crosswise into two equal pieces. Sew pieces together lengthwise to make one 63" x 80" (approximate) backing piece. Press and trim to 63" x 75".

2. Referring to Layering the Quilt on page 94, arrange and baste backing, batting, and top together. Hand or machine quilt as desired.

3. Refer to Binding the Quilt on page 94. Sew 2¾" x 42" binding strips end-to-end to make one continuous 2¾"-wide binding strip. Bind quilt to finish.

Sand CANDLES

Sand, sunshine, and summertime celebrations just seem to go together! Carry this concept to your table with this fun and easy decoration.

1. Make sure hurricanes are clean and dry.

2. Carefully pour a small amount of blue sand in bottom of hurricane, covering the bottom. Alternate pouring white and blue sand into the hurricane, making sure that sands don't mix and that stripes are visible through the glass.

3. Fill to point desired, then add red candle to complete the decoration.

Materials Needed

Glass Hurricanes (Any Size or Shape)
Red Candles to Fit Hurricanes
White and Blue Craft Sand

Americana
WALL QUILT

Americana Wall Quilt Finished Size: 38½" x 38½"	FIRST CUT		SECOND CUT	
	Number of Strips or Pieces	Dimensions	Number of Pieces	Dimensions
Fabric A Star Background ⅜ yard	1	12" x 42"	2 1	12" squares 11" square
Fabric B Corner Star Background ⅜ yard	1	12" x 42"	2	12" squares
Fabric C Center Block Corners & Stripe Block ⅝ yard	1 8	3½" x 42" 2" x 42"	4	3½" squares
Fabric D Center Block Accent & Stripe Block Medium ½ yard	1 4	5" x 42" 2" x 42"	4	5" squares
Fabric E Stripe Block Light ⅛ yard	2	2" x 42"		
First Border ¼ yard	4	1¼" x 42"	2 2	1¼" x 33½" 1¼" x 32"
Outside Border 1¼ yards (Directional) OR ⅜ yard	4	2¾" x Length of Fabric 45" (Stripe runs parallel to selvage) OR		
	4	2¾" x 42" (Non-Directional)	2 2	2¾" x 38" 2¾" x 33½"
Binding ⅜ yard	4	2¾" x 42"		
Star Appliqués - ¼ yard Backing - 1⅙ yards Batting - 42" x 42" Lightweight Fusible Web - ½ yard				

Fabric Requirements and Cutting Instructions

Read all instructions before beginning and use ¼"-wide seam allowances throughout. Read Cutting Strips and Pieces on page 92 prior to cutting fabric.

Getting Started

Stars and stripes create a dazzling patriotic display for any area in your home. Blocks measure 11" square (unfinished). Refer to Accurate Seam Allowance on page 92. Whenever possible use Assembly Line Method on page 92. Press seams in direction of arrows.

Making the Blocks

1. Refer to Quick Corner Triangles on page 92. Making quick corner triangle units, sew four 5" Fabric D squares to one 11" Fabric A piece as shown. Press. Making quick corner triangle units, sew four 3½" Fabric C squares to unit as shown. Press. Label this Center Block.

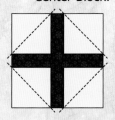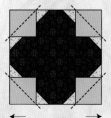

Fabric D = 5 x 5
Fabric C = 3½ x 3½
Fabric A = 11 x 11

2. Draw a diagonal line on wrong side of one 12" Fabric A square. Place marked square and one 12" Fabric B square right sides together. Sew scant ¼" away from drawn line on both sides to make half-square triangles as shown. Make two. Cut on drawn line. Press. This will make four half-square triangle units.

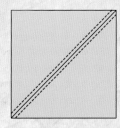

Fabric A = 12 x 12
Fabric B = 12 x 12
Make 2

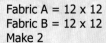
Make 4
Half-square Triangles

Show your colors and add a touch of Americana to your summertime home with this clever and quick quilt. Easy techniques bring out the stars for an All-American wall quilt.

3. Draw a diagonal line on wrong side of one unit from step 2. Place marked piece and another half-square triangle unit right sides together positioning Fabric A section on top of Fabric B section. Sew scant ¼" away from drawn line on both sides as shown. Make two. Cut on drawn line. Refer to Twisting Seams on page 92. Press. This will make four quarter-square triangle units. Square blocks to 11". Label these Corner Blocks.

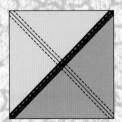

Make 2

Square to 11"
Make 4
Quarter-square Triangles

4. Sew together lengthwise four 2" x 42" Fabric C strips, two 2" x 42" Fabric D strips, and one 2" x 42" Fabric E strip (this is the center strip) as shown. Press seams toward center. Make two. Cut strip sets into four 11"-wide segments. Label this Stripe Block.

11

Make 2
Cut 4 segments

5. Sew one Stripe Block between two Corner Blocks as shown. Press. Make two.

Make 2

6. Sew Center Block between two Stripe Blocks as shown. Press.

7. Referring to photo on page 27 and layout, sew row from step 6 between two rows from step 5. Press.

Adding the Appliqué

Refer to appliqué instructions on page 93. Our instructions are for Quick-Fuse Appliqué, but if you prefer hand appliqué add ¼"-wide seam allowances.

1. Use star pattern to trace five stars on paper side of fusible web. Use appropriate fabric to prepare all appliqués for fusing.

2. Refer to photo on page 27 and layout to position and fuse appliqués to quilt. Finish appliqué edges with machine satin stitch or other decorative stitching as desired.

Adding the Borders

1. Sew quilt top between two 1¼" x 32" First Border strips. Press toward border. Sew this unit between two 1¼" x 33½" First Border strips. Press.

2. If using a directional fabric for Outside Border, refer to Mitered Borders on page 94. Sew 45" x 2¾" Outside Border strips to top, bottom, and sides of quilt, mitering corners. Press seams toward Outside Border. If using non-directional fabric refer to step 1 to sew 2¾" x 33½" and 2¾" x 38" Outside Border Strips to top, bottom, and sides of quilt.

Layering and Finishing

1. Referring to Layering the Quilt on page 94, arrange and baste backing, batting, and top together. Hand or machine quilt as desired.

2. Refer to Binding the Quilt on page 94. Using 2¾"-wide binding strips, bind quilt to finish.

Americana Wall Quilt
Finished Size: 38½" x 38½"

Star Appliqué

Tracing Line_____

Americana Wall Quilt
Make 5

Nine-Patch Pillow
Make 1

Lone Star Pillow
Make 1

Americana Door Banner
Make 1

Nine-Patch PILLOW

Nine-Patch Pillow Finished Size: 15½" square	FIRST CUT	
	Number of Strips or Pieces	Dimensions
Fabric A Background ⅓ yard	1	8½" square
Fabric B Dark Border & Backing ½ yard	2 2 1 2	10¾" x 16" 1¾" x 42" 1¾" x 16" 1¾" x 10"
Fabric C Light Border ¼ yard	1 2 1	1¾" x 42" 1¾" x 16" 1¾" x 10"
Star Appliqué - Scrap Lining - ½ yard Batting - 18" x 18" Pillow Form - 15½" Pillow Form Fabric (Optional) - ½ yard Two 16" squares Polyester Fiberfill (Optional)		

Finished Size: 15½" square

Pile patriotic pillows on your outdoor furniture for an instant shift to summertime mode. This striking star is set off by simple borders and nine-patch blocks.

Making the Pillow

1. Sew lengthwise one 1¾" x 42" Fabric C strip between two 1¾" x 42" Fabric B strips to make a strip set. Press seams toward Fabric B. Cut strip set into four 8½"-wide segments as shown. Repeat to sew one 1¾" x 10" Fabric C strip between two 1¾" x 10" Fabric B strips. Press. Cut into four 1¾"-wide segments.

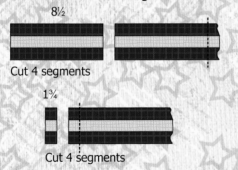

Cut 4 segments

Cut 4 segments

2. Sew lengthwise one 1¾" x 16" Fabric B strip between two 1¾" x 16" Fabric C strips to make a strip set. Press seams toward Fabric B. Cut strip set into eight 1¾"-wide segments as shown.

Cut 8 segments

3. Sew one 1¾"-wide unit from step 1 between two units from step 2 as shown. Press. Make four.

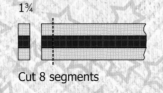

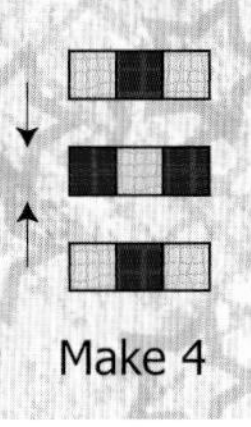

Make 4

4. Sew one 8½" Fabric A square between two 8½"-wide units from step 1. Press seams toward strip sets.

5. Sew one 8½"-wide unit from step 1 between two units from step 3. Press seams toward 8½"-wide unit. Make two.

6. Sew unit from step 4 between two units from step 5 as shown. Press.

7. Use star pattern on page 28 to trace one star on paper side of fusible web. Use appropriate fabric to prepare appliqué for fusing. Refer to photo to position and fuse appliqué to pillow. Finish appliqué edges with machine satin stitch or other decorative stitching as desired.

8. Refer to Finishing Pillows on page 94, step 1, to prepare pillow top for quilting. Quilt as desired.

9. Use two 10¾" x 16" Fabric B backing pieces and refer to Finishing Pillows, page 94, steps 2-4, to sew backing.

10. Insert 15½" pillow form or refer to Pillow Forms page 95 to make a pillow insert if desired.

Lone Star
PILLOWS

Lone Star Pillow Option 1
Finished Size: 12" square

Lone Star Pillow Option 1 Finished Size: 12" square		FIRST CUT	
		Number of Strips or Pieces	Dimensions
Fabric A Background ⅓ **yard** each of 2 Fabrics		1	10½" square *cut for each fabric
Fabric B Borders & Backing ½ yard		2	9" x 12½"
		2	3" x 12½"
		2	3" x 7½"
Fabric C Mock Piping ⅛ yard		4	1" x 7½"
Lining - ½ yard Batting - 16" x 16" Pillow Form - 12" Pillow Form Fabric (Optional) - ½ yard Two 12½" pieces Polyester Fiberfill (Optional) Star Button - 1 Note: Fabric A will make two center units one can be used for Pillow #2.			

Fabric Requirements and Cutting Instructions

Read all instructions before beginning and use ¼"-wide seam allowances throughout. Read Cutting Strips and Pieces on page 92 prior to cutting fabric. Refer to appliqué instructions on page 93 for Pillow #2. Our instructions are for Quick-Fuse Appliqué, but if you prefer hand appliqué add ¼"-wide seam allowances.

Making Pillow #1 and #2 Center Squares

1. Referring to Americana Wall Quilt on pages 26-27, steps 2 and 3, use two different 10½" Fabric A squares to make two quarter-square triangle units.

2. For Pillow #1, square quarter-square triangle unit from step 1 to 7½", square Pillow #2 quarter-square triangle unit to 9".

Making Pillow #1

1. To make a mock piping, fold four 1" x 7½" Fabric C pieces in half lengthwise wrong sides together. Press.

2. Matching raw edges, layer folded strips from step 1 on all sides of 7½" Fabric A Quarter-square Triangle unit. Baste in place.

3. Sew unit from step 2 between two 3" x 7½" Fabric B strips. Press seams toward Fabric B. Sew this unit between two 3" x 12½" Fabric B strips. Press.

4. Refer to Finishing Pillows on page 94, step 1, to prepare pillow top for quilting. Quilt as desired.

5. Use two 9" x 12½" backing pieces and refer to Finishing Pillows, page 94, steps 2-4, to sew backing.

6. Insert 12" pillow form or refer to Pillow Forms page 95 to make a pillow form if desired.

7. Sew star button to center of pillow through all layers.

You'll get two for the price of one with these cute pillows. Make both center blocks at the same time, and then finish with different colors and techniques for dramatically different looks.

Lone Star Pillow Option 2 Finished Size: 12" square	FIRST CUT	
	Number of Strips or Pieces	Dimensions
Fabric A Background 1/3 yard each of 2 Fabrics	1	10½" square *cut for each fabric
Fabric B Borders & Backing ½ yard	2 2 2	9" x 12½" 2¼" x 12½" 2¼" x 9"
Fabric C Mock Piping 1/8 yard	4	1" x 9"

Star Appliqués - Assorted scraps
Lining - ½ yard
Batting - 16" x 16"
Pillow Form - 12"
Pillow Form Fabric (Optional) - ½ yard
    Two 12½" pieces
Polyester Fiberfill (Optional)
Lightweight Fusible Web - ¼ yard

Note: Fabric A will make two center units one can be used for Pillow #1.

Tracing Line

Lone Star Pillow #2
Make 1

Star Spangled Pillow
Make 9

Making Pillow #2

1. To make a mock piping, fold four 1" x 9" Fabric C pieces in half lengthwise wrong sides together. Press.

2. Matching raw edges, layer folded strips from step 1 on all sides of 9" Fabric A quarter-square triangle unit. Baste in place.

3. Sew unit from step 2 between two 2¼" x 9" Fabric B strips. Press toward Fabric B. Sew this unit between two 2¼" x 12½" Fabric B strips. Press.

4. Use star patterns on page 28 and 31 to trace two different size stars on paper side of fusible web. Use appropriate fabric to prepare all appliqués for fusing.

5. Refer to photo to position and fuse appliqués to pillow. Finish appliqué edges with machine satin stitch or other decorative stitching as desired.

6. Refer to Finishing Pillows on page 94, step 1, to prepare pillow top for quilting. Quilt as desired.

7. Use two 9" x 12½" backing pieces and refer to Finishing Pillows, page 94, steps 2-4, to sew backing.

8. Insert 12" pillow form or refer to Pillow Forms page 95 to make a pillow form if desired.

Lone Star Pillow Option 2
Finished Size: 12" square

Americana
DOOR BANNER

Americana Door Banner Finished Size: 16" x 42"	FIRST CUT	
	Number of Strips or Pieces	Dimensions
Fabric A Star Background & Banner Stripe ½ yard	1 1	11" square 2" x 25½" (Banner Stripe)
Fabric B Block Accent & Banner Stripes ⅜ yard	4 1 1 2 2	5" squares 2" x 25½" (Banner Stripe) 1½" x 25½" (Banner Stripe) 1½" x 13" 1½" x 11"
Fabric C Block Accent & Banner Stripe ¼ yard	4 1	3½" squares 2½" x 25½" (Banner Stripe)
Fabric D Block Corner Triangles ⅓ yard	2	10" squares* *cut once diagonally
Fabric E Accent & Banner Stripe ⅙ yard	1 1	2" x 25½" (Banner Stripe) 1½" x 15½"
Fabric F Banner Stripes ⅛ yard each of 5 Fabrics	1 1 1 1 1	3½" x 25½" (Red/White) 2¼" x 25½" (Red) 1½" x 25½" (Blue) 1½" x 25½" (Tan) 1¼" x 25½" (Blue/White)
Fabric G Prairie Points & Star Appliqué ¼ yard	1 2	5" square 4" squares
Binding & Tabs ⅜ yard	3 6	2¾" x 42" 2" x 4½"

Backing - ⅝ yard (Fabric at least 44"-wide)
Batting - 20" x 44"
Lightweight Fusible Web - ¼ yard

Note: If using a directional fabric for banner stripes that runs parallel to selvage, change yardage requirement to ¾ yard.

Fabric Requirements and Cutting Instructions

Read all instructions before beginning and use ¼"-wide seam allowances throughout. Read Cutting Strips and Pieces on page 92 prior to cutting fabric.

Getting Started

Add that decorator's touch to a doorway or wall with this quick project. Refer to Accurate Seam Allowance on page 92. Whenever possible use Assembly Line Method on page 92. Press seams in direction of arrows.

Making the Banner

1. Refer to Quick Corner Triangles on page 92. Making quick corner triangle units, sew four 5" Fabric B squares to one 11" Fabric A piece as shown. Press. Sew four 3½" Fabric C squares to unit as shown. Press.

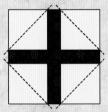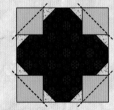

Fabric B = 5 x 5
Fabric C = 3½ x 3½
Fabric A = 11 x 11

2. Sew unit from step 1 between two 1½" x 11" Fabric B strips. Press toward Fabric B. Sew this unit between two 1½" x 13" Fabric B strips as shown. Press.

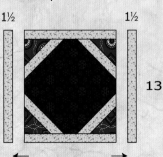

1½   1½

13

3. Sew unit from step 2 between two Fabric D triangles. Press seams toward triangles. Sew this unit between remaining Fabric D triangles. Press.

4. Referring to diagram below, measure ¼" away from each Fabric C point (red triangle) and mark as shown. Square unit connecting these marked points so unit measures 15½" square.

cut ¼" from point

Square to 15½"

5. Referring to Appliqué instructions on page 93, trace one star patter on page 28 on paper side of fusible web. Use Fabric G to prepare appliqué for fusing.

6. Refer to photo to position and fuse appliqué to center of unit from 4. Finish edges with machine satin stitch or other decorative stitching as desired.

7. Refer to photo to arrange banner strips in the following order; one 2¼" x 25½" Fabric F, 2" x 25½" Fabric B, 1½" x 25½" Fabric F, 3½" x 25½" Fabric F, 1¼" x 25½" Fabric F, 1½" x 25½" Fabric B, 2½" x 25½" Fabric C, 2" x 25½" Fabric A, 1½" x 25½" Fabric F, 2" x 25½" Fabric E. Sew strips together lengthwise. Press toward center.

Welcome friends and neighbors to the big Independence Day barbecue by hanging this star-struck banner on a gate or door. It will help set the mood for a festive and fun evening of laughter and conversation.

8. Fold and press two 4" Fabric G squares in half diagonally, wrong sides together. Fold and press diagonally in half again, as shown, to make Prairie Point. Raw edges will be together. Repeat to fold and press one 5" Fabric G square.

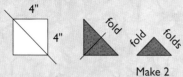

Make 2

9. Referring to photo on page 33, arrange Prairie Points on unit from step 7, placing largest in center. Baste in place.

10. Referring to photo on page 33, sew one 1½" x 15½" Fabric E strip between unit from step 6 and unit from step 7. Press toward Fabric E.

Finishing the Banner

1. Referring to Layering the Quilt on page 94, arrange and baste backing, batting, and top together. Hand or machine quilt as desired.

2. Refer to diagram below to mark bottom edge of banner at 45-degree angle to create a point.

3. Cut one 2¾" x 42" binding strip into one 2¾" x 15½" and two 12" Binding strips. Refer to binding the quilt on page 95. Sew 15½"-long binding strip to top of banner. Press. Sew one 12"-long binding strip to bottom angle line. Trim binding even with banner side edge and bottom point. Press binding away from quilt top. Sew one 12" binding strip to opposite bottom edge of quilt. Trim and press.

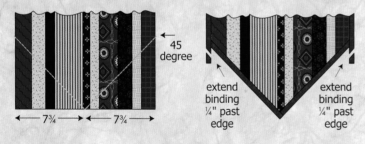

45 degree

extend binding ¼" past edge

extend binding ¼" past edge

7¾   7¾

4. Align side-binding strips even with top edge of banner. Sew strips to sides extending past bottom binding edge. Align ruler to trim side strips ¼" away from angle edge as shown. Press extension under to match angle. Press binding to the back, pin in position, and hand-stitch in place using a blind stitch.

5. Sew two 2" x 4½" tabs pieces right sides together, stitch around all sides leaving an opening for turning. Clip corners, turn, press, and hand stitch opening closed. Make three. Fold units in half, arrange and stitch to back of quilt adjusting length as desired.

Patriotic FLOWERPOT

Show your colors all summer long with this easy-to-paint flowerpot.

1. Coat flowerpot with Gesso to prepare the surface for painting. Allow flowerpot to dry thoroughly between each painting process.

2. Paint rim of flowerpot with Buttermilk paint. Two or more coats may be needed for good coverage.

3. Using ruler and pencil, mark off even stripes on flowerpot rim. Use tape to mask off areas that will remain Buttermilk. Run your thumbnail over edges of tape for good adhesion.

4. Paint Primary Red stripes on flowerpot. Remove tape while paint is still slightly wet. Allow to dry.

5. Hand-paint a Navy Blue line in the center of each Buttermilk stripe. When dry, lightly sand the rim to soften edges.

6. Paint bottom of flowerpot with Navy Blue. When thoroughly dry, spray flowerpot with several coats of varnish, following manufacturer's directions.

Materials Needed

Terracotta Flowerpot with Wide Rim

Gesso

Assorted Paintbrushes

Acrylic Craft Paints – Americana® Buttermilk and Primary Red; Delta Ceramcoat® Navy Blue

Scotch® Magic™ Tape

Ruler and Pencil

Exterior Spray Varnish

Star Spangled PILLOW

Star Spangled Pillow Finished Size: 20" square	FIRST CUT	
	Number of Strips or Pieces	Dimensions
Fabric A Background ½ yard	1	14½" square
Fabric B Borders & Backing ¾ yard	2 2 2	20½" x 13" 20½" x 3½" 3½" x 14½"

Star Appliqués - Assorted scraps
Lining - ⅔ yard
Batting - 24" x 24"
Pillow Form - 20"
Pillow Form Fabric (Optional) - ⅔ yard
    Two 20½" pieces
Polyester Fiberfill (Optional)

Cushy and comfortable, this large pillow features nine quick-fused stars on an ivory background, stipple-quilted for a fun finish.

Fabric Requirements and Cutting Instructions

Read all instructions before beginning and use ¼"-wide seam allowances throughout. Read Cutting Strips and Pieces on page 92 prior to cutting fabric. Refer to appliqué instructions on page 93. Our instructions are for Quick-Fuse Appliqué, but if you prefer hand appliqué add ¼"-wide seam allowances.

Making the Pillow

1. Sew 14½" Fabric A square between two 3½" x 14½" Fabric B strips. Press seams toward Fabric B. Sew this unit between two 20½" x 3½" Fabric B strips. Press.

2. Use Star pattern on page 31 to trace nine stars on paper side of fusible web. Use appropriate fabrics to prepare all appliqués for fusing.

3. Refer to photo to position and fuse appliqués to quilt. Finish appliqué edges with machine satin stitch or other decorative stitching as desired.

4. Refer to Finishing Pillows on page 94, step 1, to prepare pillow top for quilting. Quilt as desired.

5. Use two 20½" x 13" backing pieces and refer to Finishing Pillows, page 94, steps 2-4, to sew backing.

6. Insert 20" pillow form or refer to Pillow Forms page 95 to make a pillow form if desired.

Halloween
HAPPENINGS

Tricks & TREATS

Greet the little ghosts and goblins
with jolly jack-o'-lanterns, flickering
luminaries, and playful patchwork as
you set a boo-tiful scene for Halloween.

Black & Patch Lap Quilt

Framed Boo

Black Cat Pillow

Spooky Pillow

Boo Rocks

Luminaries

Pumpkin Table Runner

Haunted House Table Runner

Black & Patch
LAP QUILT

Black & Patch Lap Quilt Finished Size: 46½" x 56½"	FIRST CUT		SECOND CUT	
	Number of Strips or Pieces	Dimensions	Number of Pieces	Dimensions
Fabric A Background 1½ yards	8	6" x 42"	48	6" squares** **cut once diagonally
Fabric B Block Light Fabrics ⅓ yard each of 8 Fabrics	1*	4½" x 42"	6*	4½" squares** **cut once diagonally
	1*	2½" x 42"	1*	2½" x 16"
	1*	2" x 42" *cut for each fabric	2*	2" x 12"
Fabric C Block Dark Fabrics ¼ yard each of 8 Fabrics	1*	2½" x 42"	1*	2½" x 12"
	1*	2" x 42" *cut for each fabric	2*	2" x 16"
First Border ¼ yard	5	1¼" x 42"		
Outside Border ½ yard	5	2½" x 42"		
Binding ⅝ yard	6	2¾" x 42"		
Backing - 3 yards Batting - 52" x 62"				

Fabric Requirements and Cutting Instructions

Read all instructions before beginning and use ¼"-wide seam allowances throughout. Read Cutting Strips and Pieces on page 92 prior to cutting fabric.

Getting Started

Fall colors intertwine on this dazzling quilt. Extra blocks are made to allow for play of color while laying out the quilt. Use the extra blocks to make pillows to coordinate with your quilt. Blocks measure 10½" square (unfinished). Refer to Accurate Seam Allowance on page 92. Whenever possible use Assembly Line Method on page 92. Press seams in direction of arrows.

Making the Black & Patch Blocks

1. Sew one 2½" x 16" Fabric B strip between two matching 2" x 16" Fabric C strips as shown to make a strip set. Press. Make eight, each using a different combination of fabrics. Cut strip sets into forty-eight 2"-wide segments, six of each combination.

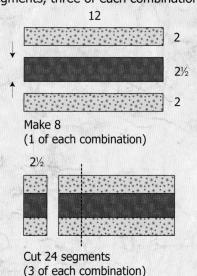

Make 8
(1 of each combination)

Cut 48 segments
(6 of each combination)

2. Using same fabric combination as step 1, sew one 2½" x 12" Fabric C strip between two 2" x 12" Fabric B strips as shown to make a strip set. Press. Make eight, each using a different combination of fabrics. Cut strip set into twenty-four 2½"-wide segments, three of each combination.

Make 8
(1 of each combination)

Cut 24 segments
(3 of each combination)

Conjure up some Halloween magic with this eye-catching quilt. Harvest colors combine with rich black for a quilt that's just-right for the entire fall season.

3. Sew one unit from step 2 between two units from step 1 as shown. Press. Make twenty-four, three of each combination.

Make 24
(3 of each combination)

4. Sew four matching Fabric B triangles to one unit from step 3 as shown. Press seams toward triangles. Note: Triangle ends extend past unit edge as shown. Make twenty-four in assorted fabric combinations.

Make 24
in assorted combinations

5. Sew four Fabric A triangles to one unit from step 4. Press. Make twenty-four. Block measures 10½" square.

Make 24 in assorted combinations
Block measures 10½" square

Assembling the Quilt

1. Refer to photo on page 39 and layout to arrange blocks in five rows. Rows 1, 3, and 5 with four blocks each and rows 2 and 4 with three whole and two partial blocks each. See step 2 before cutting blocks.

Black & Patch Lap Quilt Finished Size: 46½" x 56½"

2. Blocks on the ends of Rows 2 and 4 will be cut. Refer to diagram below to cut these blocks ¼" away from point to allow for seam allowance. Partial blocks should measure 5½" x 10½"; replace in row layout and discard smaller section.

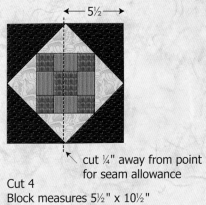

←—— 5½ ——→

cut ¼" away from point
for seam allowance

Cut 4
Block measures 5½" x 10½"

3. Sew blocks in each row together. Press seams in opposite direction from row to row. Sew rows together to make quilt center. Press.

Adding the Borders

1. Refer to Adding the Borders on page 94. Sew 1¼" x 42" First Border strips together end-to-end to make one continuous 1¼"-wide First Border strip. Measure quilt through center from side to side. Cut two 1¼"-wide First Border strips to this measurement. Sew to top and bottom of quilt. Press seams toward border.

2. Measure quilt through center from top to bottom including border just added. Cut two 1¼"-wide First Border strips to this measurement. Sew to sides of quilt. Press.

3. Refer to steps 1 and 2 to join, measure, trim, and sew 2½"-wide Outside Border strips to top, bottom, and sides of quilt. Press.

Layering and Finishing

1. Cut backing crosswise into two equal pieces. Sew pieces together lengthwise to make one 54" x 80" (approximate) backing piece. Press and trim to 54" x 62".

2. Referring to Layering the Quilt on page 94, arrange and baste backing, batting, and top together. Hand or machine quilt as desired.

3. Refer to Binding the Quilt on page 94. Sew 2¾" x 42" binding strips end-to-end to make one continuous 2¾"-wide binding strip. Bind quilt to finish.

Framed BOO

Quirky and cute, this big "BOO" is sure to be a hit in your Halloween home.

1. Apply Gesso to papier-mâché letters and allow to dry. Paint narrow sides of "B" and 9½" "O" with gloss black paint. Two or more coats may be needed for good coverage.

2. Using letters as patterns, trace "B" and large "O" on right side of fabric or paper scrap. Cut out letters on drawn line. Glue cutouts to face of prepared letters.

3. Wrap fabric scrap around shadow box back board and secure with glue. Insert 9½" "O" into shadow box and replace covered backing.

4. For 6" "O", cover cardboard matte with fabric or paper scrap. Insert matte next to glass of shadow box. Cover shadow box back board with fabric or paper and glue "O" in position desired to backing. Insert into shadow box and secure backing.

5. Display on a shelf or table for a fun Halloween accent.

Materials Needed

11½" Papier-mâché "B"

9½" Papier-mâché "O"

6" Wood "O"

Two 9¾" Square Shadow Boxes

One 9" Cardboard Matte with 5¾" Square Opening

Assorted Fabric and Paper Scraps in Halloween Colors

Gesso

Gloss Black Acrylic Paint

Assorted Paintbrushes

Permanent Adhesive Glue Stick

Black Cat
PILLOW

Fabric Requirements and Cutting Instructions

Read all instructions before beginning and use ¼"-wide seam allowances throughout. Read Cutting Strips and Pieces on page 92 prior to cutting fabric. Refer to appliqué instructions on page 93. Our instructions are for Quick-Fuse Appliqué, but if you prefer hand appliqué reverse template and add ¼"-wide seam allowances.

Making the Pillow

1. Sew 11½" Fabric A square between two 2" x 11½" Fabric B strips. Press toward Fabric B. Sew this unit between two 2" x 14½" Fabric B strips. Press.

2. Enlarge cat pattern on page 44 by 200%. Trace pattern on paper side of fusible web. Note: Pillow appliqué is a silhouette only and does not have eyes. Use appropriate fabric to prepare appliqué for fusing. Refer to photo to position and fuse appliqué to pillow. Finish appliqué edges with machine satin stitch or other decorative stitching as desired.

3. Refer to Finishing Pillows on page 94, step 1, to prepare pillow top for quilting. Quilt as desired.

4. Use two 10" x 14½" Fabric B backing pieces and refer to Finishing Pillows, page 94, steps 2-4, to sew backing.

5. Insert 14" pillow form or refer to Pillow Forms page 95 to make a pillow insert if desired.

Finished Size: 14" square

It's good luck when this black cat crosses your path! Costume your sofa for Halloween with these quick and clever pillows. Felted wool makes this cat silhouette fuzzy and fun.

Black Cat Pillow Finished Size: 14" square	FIRST CUT	
	Number of Strips or Pieces	Dimensions
Fabric A Background ⅜ yard	1	11½" square
Fabric B Outside Border ⅛ yard	2	2" x 14½"
	2	2" x 11½"

Cat Appliqué - ⅓ yard wool
Lining - ½ yard
Backing - ⅓ yard
    Two 10" x 14½"
Batting - 18" x 18"
Lightweight Fusible Web - ⅓ yard
Pillow Form - 14" square
Pillow Form Fabric (Optional) - ½ yard
    Two 14½" squares
Polyester Fiberfill (Optional)

Spooky
PILLOW

Finished Size: 5½" x 14"

Spooky Pillow Finished Size: 5½" x 14"	FIRST CUT	
	Number of Strips or Pieces	Dimensions
Wool Background and Backing ¼ yard	2	6" x 14½"

"Spooky" Appliqué - ⅛ yard
Lightweight Fusible Web - ⅛ yard
Polyester Fiberfill
Medium Black Rickrack - ⅛ yard
Wide Black Rickrack - 1⅓ yards

Create a spook-tacular look with this playful pillow. A bit of rickrack underscores the spooky theme and giant rickrack provides a photo-worthy finish.

Fabric Requirements and Cutting Instructions

Refer to appliqué instructions on page 93. Our instructions are for Quick-Fuse Appliqué, but if you prefer hand appliqué reverse template and add ¼"-wide seam allowances.

Making the Pillow

1. Use "Spooky" pattern to trace letters on paper side of fusible web. Use appropriate fabric to prepare appliqué for fusing. Refer to photo to position and fuse appliqué to pillow. Finish appliqué edges with machine satin stitch or other decorative stitching as desired.

2. Refer to photo to position and sew small rickrack to pillow top.

3. Sew wide rickrack to pillow along outside edge. Do not press rickrack to the outside. It will be sandwiched between layers when sewing backing to pillow.

4. Layer and center pillow top and backing right sides together. Using ¼"-wide seam, stitch around all edges, leaving a 4" opening on one side for turning. Clip corners, turn, and press.

5. Fill pillow with polyester fiberfill to desired fullness. Hand-stitch opening closed.

Make Two

Spooky Pillow
Patterns are reversed for use with Quick-Fuse Applique (page 93)

Tracing Line _____

BOOROCKS

Conjure up a quick centerpiece by spray painting some rocks, adding stickers, and arranging in a bowl. This centerpiece will add a touch of magic to your table.

1. Clean rocks and allow to dry.

2. Spray paint rocks with gloss black paint and allow to dry thoroughly.

3. Apply one letter sticker to each rock to spell 'BOO'. Apply jack-o'-lantern stickers to larger rocks.

4. Arrange candle, embellished rocks, and orange sea glass in bowl.

Materials Needed

Flat-Sided Rocks in Various Sizes

Gloss Black Spray Paint

'BOO' Letters and Jack-o'-Lantern Stickers

Black Candle

Black and Orange Bowl

Orange Sea Glass or Glass Gems

Jack-o'-Lantern Luminary Pattern

Cat Luminary Pattern

Black Cat Pillow

Enlarge 200% to complete pillow project.

Pattern is reversed for use with Quick-Fuse Applique (page 93)

Tracing Line_____

Permission to photocopy this page is granted by Debbie Mumm Inc. to successfully complete Black Cat Pillow.

LUMINARIES

Light up the night with grinning ghosts and jack-o'-lanterns. Tin buckets are pierced with hammer and nails, then painted. Older kids will love helping with this project!

1. Fill buckets with water and freeze for several days prior to doing this project. The ice in each bucket will keep the bucket from caving in when piercing with nail and hammer.

2. Refer to Jack-o'-Lantern, Black Cat and Ghost patterns on pages 44 and 45. Transfer patterns to paper and center each pattern on the side of a bucket. Note: We reversed cat pattern for this project.

3. Using hammer and nail, outline each figure with small nail holes. When complete, dispose of ice and dry bucket well.

4. Paint inside pierced outline with acrylic paint. Use white for the ghost, black for the cat, and orange and green for the jack-o'-lantern. Two or more coats of paint may be needed for good coverage. Allow to dry thoroughly.

5. Spray surface with gloss varnish and allow to dry.

6. Insert candles and enjoy your luminaries.

Note: Pierced design creates sharp edges inside bucket. Handle carefully. Always follow the basic rules of fire safety when burning candles.

Ghost Pattern

Materials Needed

Small Tin Buckets
(Ours are 5½" High and 6½" top diameter)

Hammer and Nails

Acrylic Craft Paints – Americana® Jack-o'-lantern Orange, Hauser Light Green, Black, and White

Assorted Paintbrushes

Gloss Spray Varnish

Votive Candles – One for each bucket

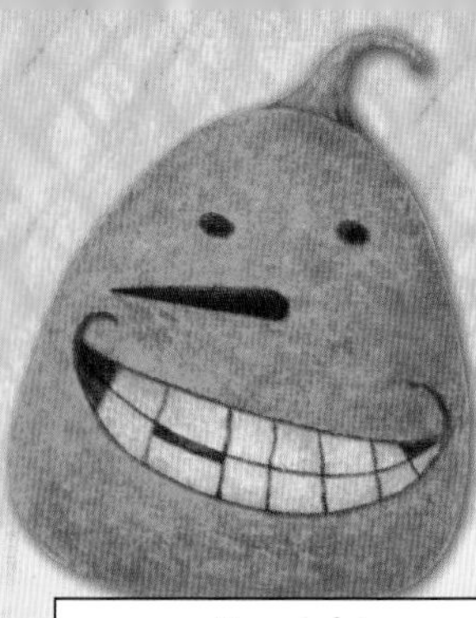

Pumpkin TABLE RUNNER

Pumpkin Table Runner Finished Size: 48" x 14"	FIRST CUT		SECOND CUT	
	Number of Strips or Pieces	Dimensions	Number of Pieces	Dimensions
Fabric A Pumpkin Background ⅓ yard	1	8½" x 42"	2	8½" squares
Fabric B Strip-Pieced Blocks, Outside Border & Prairie Points ⅓ yard each of 4 Fabrics	3*	2½" x 42" *cut for each fabric	4*	2½" squares** **extra squares are cut to allow for border placement options
Fabric C First Border ¼ yard	3	1½" x 42"	2 2	1½" x 40½" 1½" x 10½"
Pumpkin Appliqué - ¼ yard Appliqués - Assorted scraps Backing - 1 yard Batting - 52" x 18" Lightweight Fusible Web - ¼ yard Jumbo Rickrack (Optional) - 2¾ yards				

Fabric Requirements and Cutting Instructions

Read all instructions before beginning and use ¼"-wide seam allowances throughout. Read Cutting Strips and Pieces on page 92 prior to cutting fabric.

Getting Started

Set the scene for Halloween with a table runner that adds color and whimsy to your table. Blocks measure 8½" square (unfinished). Refer to Accurate Seam Allowance on page 92. Whenever possible use the Assembly Line Method on page 92. Press seams in direction of arrows.

Making the Pumpkin Block

Refer to appliqué instructions on page 93. Our instructions are for Quick-Fuse Appliqué, but if you prefer hand appliqué, reverse templates and add ¼"-wide seam allowances.

1. Use pattern on page 48 to trace two pumpkins on paper side of fusible web. Use appropriate fabrics to prepare all appliqués for fusing.

2. Refer to photo on page 47 and layout on page 48 to position and fuse appliqués to 8½" Fabric A squares. Finish appliqué edges with machine satin stitch or other decorative stitching as desired.

Making the Strip-Pieced Block

1. Sew together lengthwise four 2½" x 42" Fabric B strips, one of each fabric, to make a strip set. Press seams in one direction. Make two. Cut strip sets into three 8½"-wide segments for Strip-Pieced Block.

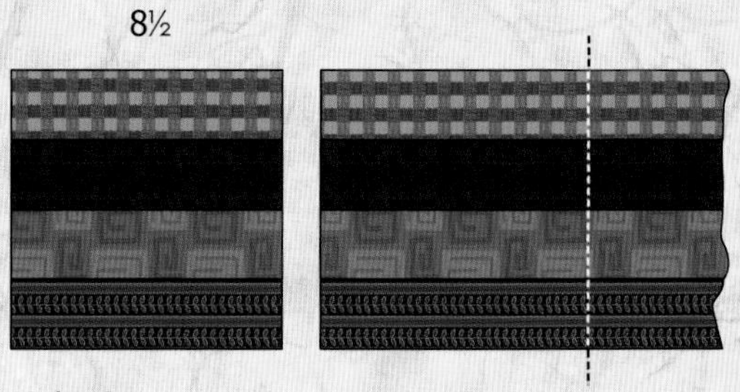

Make 2
Cut 3 segments

2. Cut fourteen 2½"-wide segments from remaining strip set to use for Outside Border.

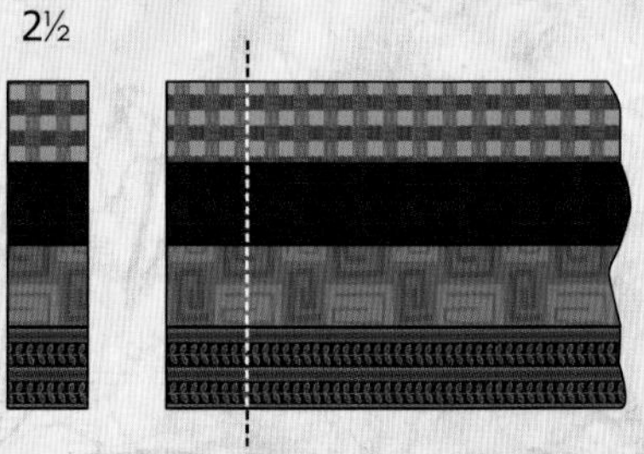

Cut 14 segments

Assembling the Table Runner

1. Refer to photo on page 47 and layout on page 48 to arrange and sew together three Strip-Pieced Blocks and two Pumpkin Blocks. Press seams toward Pumpkin Blocks.

2. Sew unit from step 1 between two 1½" x 40½" Fabric C strips. Press seams toward border. Sew this unit between two 1½" x 10½" Fabric C strips. Press.

Treat your family and friends to a fun-loving Halloween full of color and texture and all your favorite spooky characters. This table runner features pumpkins, but can be easily adapted for other appliqués or fabric panels.

3. Refer to photo and layout on page 48 to arrange 2½"-wide segments for outside border. Some units will need to be unstitched to obtain the appropriate lengths and arrangements. Top and bottom units will use five units plus one square. Side borders will use one 2½"-wide unit plus three squares.

4. Sew unit from step 2 between two longer units from step 3. Press. Sew this unit between two smaller units from step 3. Press.

5. Fold one 2½" Fabric B square in half diagonally wrong sides together. Fold again in half diagonally as shown. Press. Make fourteen Prairie Points to match outside side edges of quilt.

6. Referring to layout on page 48, align prairie points along quilt outside side edges matching fabric used and raw edges as shown. Baste in place.

Finishing the Table Runner

1. Cut backing crosswise into two equal pieces. Sew pieces together lengthwise to make one 18" x 80" (approximate) backing piece. Press and trim to 18" x 52".

2. Layer and center table runner and backing right sides together on batting, wrong side of backing on batting. Using ¼"-wide seam, stitch around all edges, leaving a 4" opening on one side for turning. Trim batting close to stitching and backing even with quilt edges. Clip corners, turn, and press. Hand-stitch opening closed.

3. Machine or hand quilt as desired. Refer to photo above and add rickrack to quilt. Embellish as desired.

Pumpkin Table Runner Finished Size: 48" x 14"

Pumpkin Table Runner

Tracing Line —————————
Tracing Line ·······················
(will be hidden behind other fabrics)

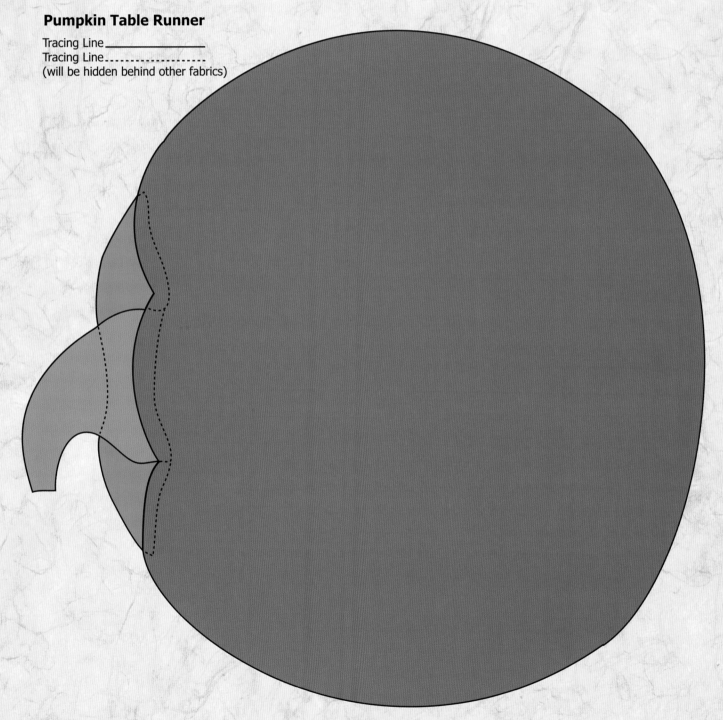

Haunted House
TABLE RUNNER

Use a Halloween motif fabric to make this runner even simpler and more spook-tacular!

Making the Table Runner

1. Refer to Halloween Pumpkin Table Runner on page 46, Making the Strip-Pieced Block step 1 to make one strip set and cut three 8½" segments.

2. Referring to photo, arrange and sew together three Strip-Pieced Blocks and two 8½" Fabric A squares. Press seams toward Fabric A.

3. Sew unit from step 2 between two 1½" x 40½" Fabric C strips. Press seams toward border. Sew this unit between two 1½" x 10½" Fabric C strips. Press.

4. Cut two 2½" x 14½" Fabric D strips. Sew remaining strips together end-to-end to make one continuous 2½"-wide strip.

5. Measure quilt through center from side to side. Cut two 2½"-wide Fabric D strips to this measurement. Sew to top and bottom of quilt. Press seams toward border.

6. Sew 2½" x 14½" Fabric D strips to sides. Press.

Materials Needed

Fabric A: (Halloween Motif) ⅓ yard
   Two 8½" squares
Fabric B: (Strip-Pieced Blocks) ⅛ yard each of 4 fabrics
   One 2½" x 42" strip for each fabric
Fabric C: First Border - ¼ yard
   Two 1½" x 40½" strips
   Two 1½" x 10½" strips
Fabric D: (Outside Border) ⅓ yard
   Three 2½" x 42" strips
Binding - ⅓ yard
   Three 2¾" x 42" strips
Backing - 1 yard
Batting - 52" x 18"
Jumbo Rickrack - 2¾ yards (optional)

Layering and Finishing

1. Refer to Finishing the Table Runner, step 1, page 47 to piece and cut backing.

2. Referring to Layering the Quilt on page 94, arrange and baste backing, batting, and top together. Hand or machine quilt as desired. Refer to photo to add rickrack to quilt.

3. Refer to Binding the Quilt on page 94. Sew 2¾" x 42" binding strips end-to-end to make one continuous 2¾"-wide binding strip. Bind quilt to finish.

Harvest
CELEBRATIONS

Happy HOMECOMINGS

Whether it's a football game, barn dance, or Thanksgiving dinner, welcome family and friends with colorful quilts, beautiful banners, delicious food, and warm hospitality.

Autumn Abundance
WALL QUILT

Materials Needed

Fabric A Background - ½ yard
    One 16½" x 24" piece

Fabric B Tablecloth - ⅓ yard
    One 8½" x 24" piece

Basket Lining (Optional for woven basket) - ⅓ yard
    One 10" square
(Note: This should be a similar color to basket.)

Appliqué Woven Basket - ¼ yard
    One 6½" x 16" piece

Appliqué Vegetables - Assorted wool
    and/or cotton scraps

Lightweight fusible web - ⅔ yard

Fusible Interfacing - ⅔ yard
    One 24" square

Binding - ¼ yard
    Three 2¼" x 42" strips

Backing - ⅔ yard

Batting - 22" x 22"

Optional Framed Finish
Materials Needed
Picture Frame - 18" to 20" square
Acid Free Mat Board - to fit inside frame opening

Cut mat board to frame opening size, wrap quilt around mat, and finish as desired. Insert into frame.

Getting Started

This elegant wallhanging accents any décor for autumn while celebrating the richness of the season.

1. Sew 8½" x 24" Fabric B piece to 16½" x 24" Fabric A piece using ¼"-wide seam allowance. Press.

2. Referring to manufacturer's instructions, fuse iron-on interfacing to wrong side of unit from step one.

Adding the Appliqués

Refer to appliqué instructions on page 93. Our instructions are for Quick-Fuse Appliqué, but if you prefer hand appliqué, reverse templates and add ¼"-wide seam allowance.

1. Use patterns on pages 54-57 to trace Autumn Abundance appliqués on paper side of fusible web. Use appropriate fabrics to prepare all appliqués for fusing. Note: Patterns are on four pages, align placement lines to trace a complete pattern.

2. For woven basket, refer to manufacturers instructions to fuse lightweight fusible web to 6½" x 16" basket fabric. Cut into ½"-wide strips.

3. Trace basket shape on lining fabric to be used as a base. Weave cut strips over drawn basket area. Fuse in place. Cut out basket on drawn line.

4. For sides of basket, trim ½"-wide cut strips slightly narrower and fuse over woven basket side edges.

5. Referring to Couching on page 95, attach yarn following gourd stitching lines.

6. Refer to photo to arrange and fuse appliqués to background. Finish appliqué edges with machine blanket stitch or other decorative stitching as desired.

7. Referring to photo and pattern pieces, hand or machine embroider wheat beards and stems to quilt.

Finishing

1. Layer top, batting, and backing together. Quilt as desired. Trim to desired size.

2. Refer to Binding the Quilt on page 94. Using 2¼"-wide binding strips, bind to finish. Note: Binding finishes ¼"-wide instead of our normal ½"-wide.

Leaves are falling and pumpkins line the porch steps. Welcome them home with wall art that reflects the warmth and color of the changing season. A mix of wool and cotton appliqués create a texture-rich scene and two different finishing techniques provide plenty of options.

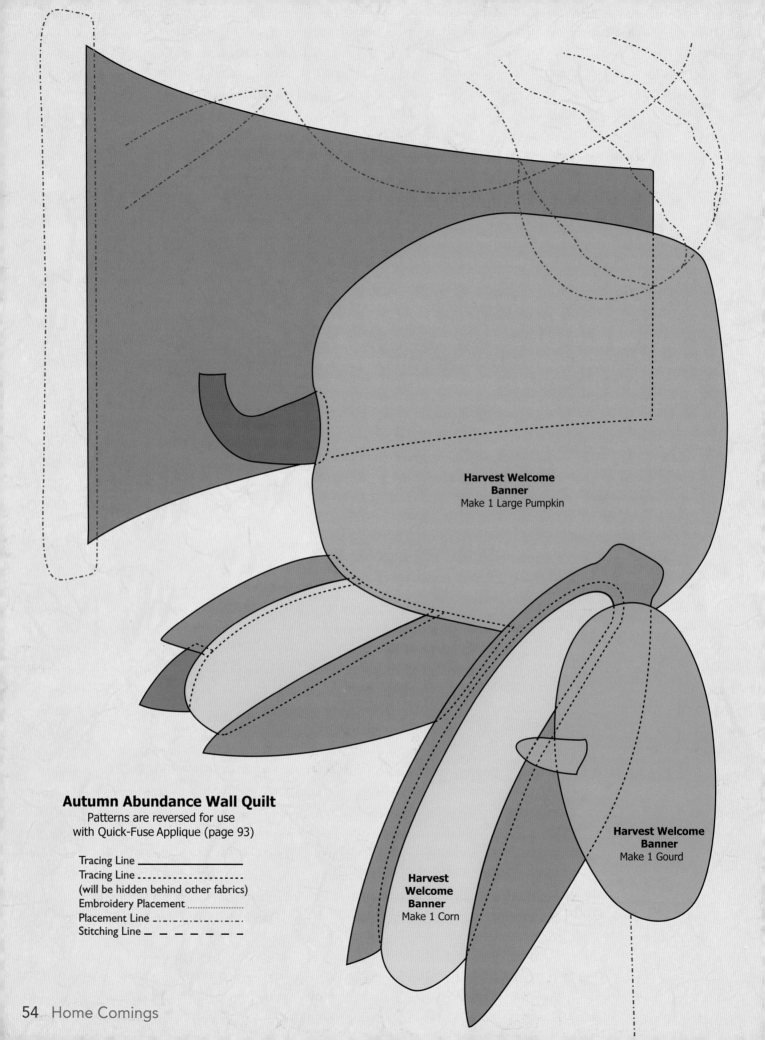

Harvest Welcome Banner
Make 1 Large Pumpkin

Harvest Welcome Banner
Make 1 Gourd

Harvest Welcome Banner
Make 1 Corn

Autumn Abundance Wall Quilt
Patterns are reversed for use
with Quick-Fuse Applique (page 93)

Tracing Line ⎯⎯⎯⎯⎯⎯⎯
Tracing Line ·····················
(will be hidden behind other fabrics)
Embroidery Placement ················
Placement Line ·–··–··–··–··–·
Stitching Line ⎯ ⎯ ⎯ ⎯ ⎯

Autumn Abundance Wall Quilt
Make 1 of each pattern piece

**Harvest Welcome
Banner**
Make 1 Medium Pumpkin

Appliqué Pressing Sheet (page 93) is recommended for this project
to fuse appliqué pieces together to make a larger unit.

Autumn Abundance Wall Quilt

Patterns are reversed for use
with Quick-Fuse Applique (page 93)

Tracing Line ―――――――――
Tracing Line --------------------
(will be hidden behind other fabrics)
Embroidery Placement ....
Placement Line ---·---·---·---·

Autumn Abundance Wall Quilt
Make 1 of each pattern piece

Appliqué Placement Guide

Harvest
LAP QUILT

Harvest Lap Quilt Finished Size: 49½" x 57½"	FIRST CUT		SECOND CUT	
	Number of Strips or Pieces	Dimensions	Number of Pieces	Dimensions
Fabric A Lights ½ yard each of 5 Fabrics	1* 3*	4½" x 42" 2½" x 42" *cut for each fabric	3* 18* 9*	4½" squares 2½" x 4½" 2½" squares
Fabric B Mediums ½ yard each of 6 Fabrics	1* 3*	4½" x 42" 2½" x 42" *cut for each fabric	2* 14* 7*	4½" squares 2½" x 4½" 2½" squares
Fabric C Darks ⅓ yard each of 4 Fabrics	1* 2*	4½" x 42" 2½" x 42" *cut for each fabric	6* 21*	4½" squares 2½" squares
Wide Binding ¾ yard	7	3½" x 42"		
Backing - 3⅛ yards Batting - 56" x 64"				

Fabric Requirements and Cutting Instructions

Read all instructions before beginning and use ¼"-wide seam allowances throughout. Read Cutting Strips and Pieces on page 92 prior to cutting fabric.

Getting Started

Stay warm on those crisp cold fall days wrapped in this lustrous quilt showcasing the colors of the season. Blocks measure 8½" square (unfinished). Refer to Accurate Seam Allowance on page 92. Whenever possible use Assembly Line Method on page 92. Press seams in direction of arrows.

Making the Harvest Block

This scrappy quilt uses a variety of colors and shades to achieve the dramatic diagonal stripe. Refer to our quilt for inspiration when laying out your creation. Pick fabric pieces at random, sew them into blocks, and then arrange blocks to create this quilt.

1. Sew one 2½" x 4½" Fabric A piece between two 2½" Fabric A squares as shown. Press. Make twenty-two using assorted fabrics.

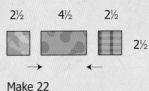

2½"   4½"   2½"

2½"

Make 22

2. Sew one 4½" Fabric A square between two 2½" x 4½" Fabric A pieces. Press. Make eleven using assorted fabrics.

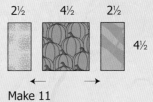

2½"   4½"   2½"

4½"

Make 11

3. Sew one unit from step 2 between two units from step 1 as shown. Press. Make eleven using assorted fabrics. Label these Light Blocks. Blocks measure 8½" square.

Light Block

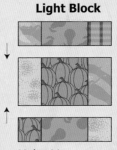

Make 11
Block meaures 8½" square

4. Refer to steps 1-3 and use assorted Fabric B squares and pieces to make blocks. Press. Make ten using assorted fabrics. Label these Medium Blocks. Blocks measure 8½" square.

2½"   4½"   2½"

2½"

Make 20

2½"   4½"   2½"

4½"

Make 10

Medium Block

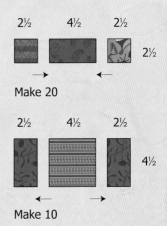

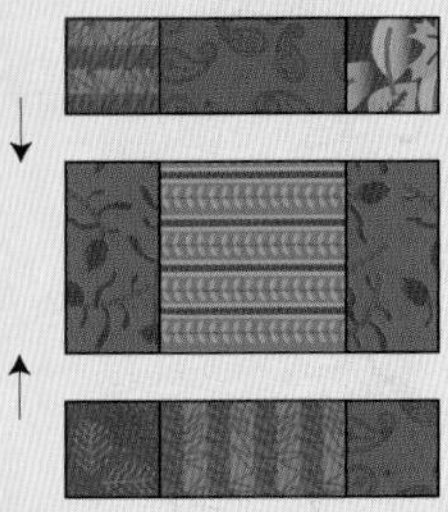

Make 10
Block meaures 8½" square

The glorious colors of autumn march in a dramatic diagonal pattern across this simply sensational lap quilt that will bring instant autumn ambiance to your home. A single, simple, block creates this stunning quilt.

5. Sew one 2½" x 4½" Fabric A piece between two 2½" Fabric C squares as shown. Press. Make twenty-one using assorted Fabric A and C pieces. Make twenty-one using assorted 2½" x 4½" Fabric B pieces and 2½" Fabric C squares.

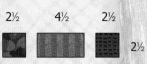

2½   4½   2½

2½

← →

Make 42
21 using Fabric A/C combination
21 using Fabric B/C combination

6. Sew one 4½" Fabric C square between one 2½" x 4½" Fabric A piece and one 2½" x 4½" Fabric B piece. Press. Make twenty-one using assorted fabrics.

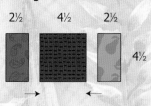

2½   4½   2½

4½

→ ←

Make 21

7. Sew one unit from step 6 between two units from step 5 as shown. Press. Make twenty-one and label these Mixed Blocks. Blocks measure 8½" square.

Mixed Block

Make 21
Block meaures
8½" square

Layering and Finishing

1. Refer to photo on page 59 and layout to arrange Light, Medium and Mixed Blocks in seven rows with six blocks each. Rotate Mixed Blocks as necessary to create diagonal color pattern.

2. Sew blocks together pressing seams in opposite direction from row to row. Sew rows together. Press.

3. Cut backing crosswise into two equal pieces. Sew pieces together lengthwise to make one 56" x 80" (approximate) backing piece. Press and trim to 56" x 64".

4. Referring to Layering the Quilt on page 94, arrange and baste backing, batting, and top together. Hand or machine quilt as desired.

5. Refer to Binding the Quilt on page 94. Sew 3½" x 42" binding strips end-to-end to make one continuous 3½"-wide binding strip. Cut backing and batting ½" beyond raw edge of quilt top. This will add fullness to the ¾"-wide finished binding. Bind quilt to finish.

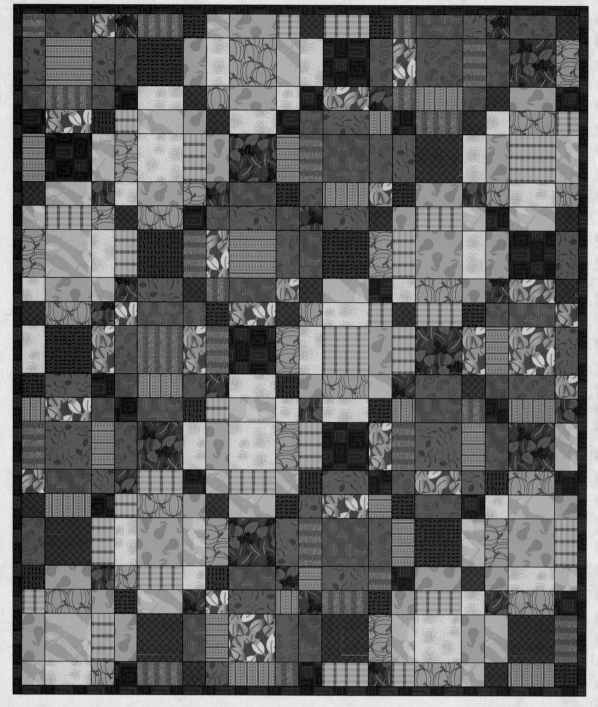

Harvest Lap Quilt
Finished Size: 49½" x 57½"

Harvest
TABLE QUILT

Getting Started

This multi-colored table quilt is a great companion to the Harvest Quilt. Blocks measure 8½" square (unfinished). Refer to Accurate Seam Allowance on page 92. Whenever possible use Assembly Line Method on page 92. Press seams in direction of arrows.

Making the Table Quilt

1. Sew 23" Fabric D square between two 1¼" x 23" Fabric E strips. Press toward Fabric E. Sew this unit between two 1¼" x 24½" Fabric E strips. Press.

2. Refer to Harvest Quilt page 58-60, Making the Harvest Block steps 1-7 to make four Light Blocks, four Medium Blocks, and eight Mixed Blocks.

3. Referring to photo below, sew one Light Block between two Mixed Blocks. Press away from center. Make four.

4. Sew unit from step 1 between two units from step 3. Press toward center.

5. Referring to photo below, arrange and sew one unit from step 3 between two Medium Blocks. Press. Make two.

6. Sew unit from step 4 between units from step 5. Press.

Harvest Table Quilt Finished Size: 41" x 41"	FIRST CUT		SECOND CUT	
	Number of Strips or Pieces	Dimensions	Number of Pieces	Dimensions
Fabric A Lights ⅓ yard each of 5 Fabrics	1*	4½" square		
	2*	2½" x 42" *cut for each fabric	7*	2½" x 4½"
			4*	2½" squares
Fabric B Mediums ¼ yard each of 7 Fabrics	1*	4½" square		
	1*	2½" x 42" *cut for each fabric	5*	2½" x 4½"
			3*	2½" squares
Fabric C Darks ¼ yard each of 4 Fabrics	1*	4½" x 42"	2*	4½" squares
	1*	2½" x 42" *cut for each fabric	8*	2½" squares
Fabric D Center ¾ yard	1	23" x 42"	1	23" square
Fabric E Accent Border ¼ yard	4	1¼" x 42"	2	1¼" x 24½"
			2	1¼" x 23"
Binding ½ yard	4**	2¾" x 42" **If strip measures less than 41" - cut five.		

Backing - 2⅝ yards
Flannel or Lightweight Batting - 47" x 47"

7. Cut backing crosswise into two equal pieces. Sew pieces together lengthwise to make one 47" x 80" (approximate) backing pieces. Press and trim to 47" x 47".

8. Referring to Layering the Quilt on page 94, arrange and baste backing, batting, and top together. Hand or machine quilt as desired.

9. Refer to Binding the Quilt on page 94. Using four 2¾" x 42" binding strips, bind quilt to finished. If strips measure less than 41", sew five 2¾" x 42" binding strips end-to-end to make one continuous 2¾"-wide binding strip. Bind quilt to finish.

Serve them hot soup and crunchy rolls as you celebrate the abundance of the season with a table quilt that's as spicy and heart-warming as the food. Pick a favorite iconic fabric for the center and surround it with the beautiful Harvest Block border.

Harvest Table Quilt
Finished Size: 41" x 41"

Thanksgiving
TABLE QUILT

Thanksgiving Table Quilt Finished Size: 41" x 41"	FIRST CUT		SECOND CUT	
	Number of Strips or Pieces	Dimensions	Number of Pieces	Dimensions
Fabric A Center ¾ yard	1	23" x 42"	1	23" square
Fabric B Accent Border ¼ yard	4	1¼" x 42"	2 2	1¼" x 24½" 1¼" x 23"
Fabric C Border Background 1⅛ yards	8	4½" x 42"	64	4½" squares
Fabric D Border Accent Squares ⅓ yard each of 6 Fabrics	1*	8½" x 42" *cut for each fabric	3*	8½" squares
Binding ½ yard	4**	2¾" x 42" **If strip measures less than 41" - cut five.		
Backing - 2⅝ yards Flannel or Lightweight Batting - 47" x 47"				

Fabric Requirements and Cutting Instructions

Read all instructions before beginning and use ¼"-wide seam allowances throughout. Read Cutting Strips and Pieces on page 92 prior to cutting fabric.

Getting Started

These simple blocks add color and interest to the rich centerpiece in this table quilt. Border block measures 8½" square (unfinished). Refer to Accurate Seam Allowance on page 92. Whenever possible use Assembly Line Method on page 92. Press seams in direction of arrows.

Making the Table Quilt

Blocks are made with a variety of Fabric D fabrics, two extra were cut to allow for placement options.

1. Refer to Quick Corner Triangles on page 92. Making quick corner triangle units, sew four 4½" Fabric C squares to one 8½" Fabric D square as shown. Press. Make sixteen in assorted Fabric D fabrics.

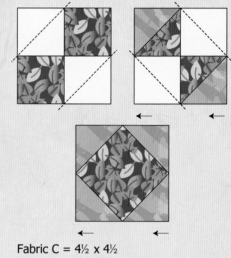

Fabric C = 4½ x 4½
Fabric D = 8½ x 8½
Make 16

2. Sew 23" Fabric A square between two 1¼" x 23" Fabric B strips. Press seams toward Fabric B. Sew this unit between two 1¼" x 24½" Fabric B strips. Press.

Thanksgiving Table Quilt
Finished Size: 41" x 41"

Gather your family at a table that's dressed in the vibrant colors of a sunny fall day. Simple piecing creates a border to showcase one of your favorite fabrics.

3. Referring to photo and layout on page 62, arrange and sew together three blocks from step 1. Press. Make two. Sew to top and bottom of unit from step 2. Press.

4. Referring to photo and layout on page 62, arrange and sew together five blocks from step 1. Press. Make two. Sew to sides of unit from step 3. Press.

5. Cut backing crosswise into two equal pieces. Sew pieces together lengthwise to make one 47" x 80" (approximate) backing piece. Press and trim to 47" x 47".

6. Referring to Layering the Quilt on page 94, arrange and baste backing, flannel, and top together. Flannel is being substituted for batting to keep quilt lightweight and it will allow the quilt to drape nicely. Hand or machine quilt as desired. Pre-washing flannel is recommended to reduce shrinkage.

7. Refer to Binding the Quilt on page 94. Using four 2¾" x 42" binding strips, bind quilt to finish. If strips measure less than 41", sew five 2¾" x 42" binding strips end-to-end to make one continuous 2¾"-wide binding strip. Bind quilt to finish.

Pumpkins in a Row
WALL QUILT

Pumpkins in a Row Wall Quilt Finished Size: 33" x 21"	FIRST CUT		SECOND CUT	
	Number of Strips or Pieces	Dimensions	Number of Pieces	Dimensions
Fabric A Background ½ yard	1	5½" x 42"	1	5½" x 19½"
	1	3½" x 42"	2	3½" squares
			2	3½" x 3"
			4	2½" squares
	1	2" x 42"	1	2" x 6½"
			2	2" x 3"
			6	2" squares
	1	1½" x 42"	1	1½" x 6½"
			2	1½" x 3½"
			8	1½" squares
Fabric B Pumpkin Unit 1 ⅓ yard	1	8½" x 12½"		
Fabric C Pumpkin Unit 2 ¼ yard	1	6½" x 7½"		
Fabric D Pumpkin Unit 3 ¼ yard	1	7½" x 9½"		
Fabric E Pumpkin Unit 4 ¼ yard	1	6½" square		
Fabric F Stems Assorted scraps	1	2½" x 3½"		
	1	1½" x 3½"		
	1	1½" x 2"		
	1	1½" square		
Fabric G - Gold ⅛ yard	1	2½" x 42"	2	2½" x 4½"
			2	2½" x 3½"
			1	2½" square
Fabric G - Dk Green ⅛ yard	1	2½" x 42"	1	2½" x 4½"
			5	2½" squares
Fabric G - Lt Green ⅛ yard	1	2½" x 42"	1	2½" x 4½"
			3	2½" squares
Fabric G - Orange ⅛ yard	1	2½" x 42"	1	2½" x 5½"
			2	2½" x 3½"
Fabric G - Orange/ Yellow ⅛ yard	1	2½" x 42"	2	2½" x 4½"
			1	2½" x 3½"
			1	2½" square
Fabric G - Brown ⅛ yard	1	2½" x 42"	4	2½" x 5½"
			2	2½" x 3½"
			3	2½" squares
Accent Border ⅙ yard	3	1" x 42"	2	1" x 27½"
			2	1" x 16½"
Binding ⅜ yard	4	2¾" x 42"		

Backing - ¾ yard
Batting - 37" x 25"
"Pumpkin" & Leaf Appliqués - Assorted scrap
Yarn (Pumpkin Vine) - ⅓ yard
Lightweight Fusible Web - ⅙ yard

Fabric Requirements and Cutting Instructions

Read all instructions before beginning and use ¼"-wide seam allowances throughout. Read Cutting Strips and Pieces on page 92 prior to cutting fabric.

Getting Started

This wall quilt is an easy project to make for the season. The pieced border adds just the right accent to the wallhanging and reflects the colors of the season. Refer to Accurate Seam Allowance on page 92. Whenever possible use Assembly Line Method on page 92. Press seams in direction of arrows.

Making the Wall Quilt

1. Refer to Quick Corner Triangles on page 92. Making a quick corner triangle unit, sew one 1½" Fabric A square to one 2½" x 3½" Fabric F piece as shown. Press.

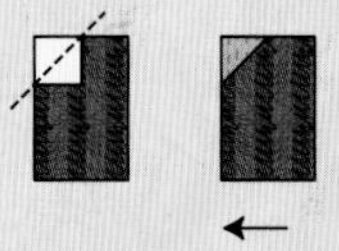

Fabric A = 1½ x 1½
Fabric F = 2½ x 3½

2. Sew unit from step 1 between two 3½" Fabric A squares as shown. Press.

3½   3½

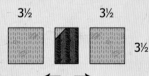

3½

3. Making quick corner triangle units, sew four 2½" Fabric A squares to one 8½" x 12½" Fabric B piece as shown. Press.

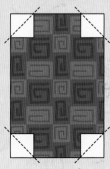

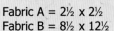

Fabric A = 2½ x 2½
Fabric B = 8½ x 12½

Pretty pumpkins line up to greet visitors in this whimsical wall quilt. A scrappy border and dimensional embellishments make this quilt a seasonal favorite.

4. Sew unit from step 2 to unit from step 3 together as shown. Press and label this Unit 1.

Unit 1

5. Sew one 1½" x 2" Fabric F piece between two 2" x 3" Fabric A pieces as shown. Press.

3   1½   3

   2

6. Making quick corner triangle units, sew four 2" Fabric A squares to 6½" x 7½" Fabric C piece as shown. Press.

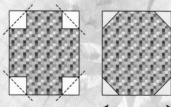

Fabric A = 2 x 2
Fabric C = 6½ x 7½

7. Sew unit from step 5 between one 2" x 6½" Fabric A piece and unit from step 5 as shown. Press and label this Unit 2.

Unit 2

6½

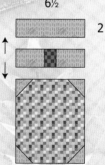

2

8. Sew one 1½" Fabric F square between two 1½" x 3½" Fabric A pieces as shown. Press.

3½   1½   3½

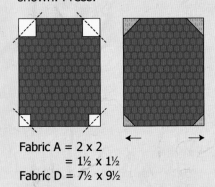 1½

9. Making quick corner triangle units, sew two 2" Fabric A squares and two 1½" Fabric A squares to one 7½" x 9½" Fabric D piece as shown. Press.

Fabric A = 2 x 2
         = 1½ x 1½
Fabric D = 7½ x 9½

10. Sew unit from step 8 to unit from step 9 together as shown. Press and label Unit 3.

Unit 3

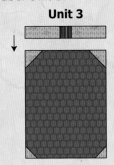

11. Making a quick corner triangle unit, sew one 1½" Fabric A square to one 1½" x 3½" Fabric F piece as shown. Press.

Fabric A = 1½ x 1½
Fabric F = 1½ x 3½

12. Sew unit from step 11 between two 3½" x 3" Fabric A pieces as shown. Press.

3   3

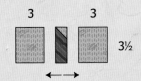 3½

13. Making quick corner triangle units, sew four 1½" Fabric A squares to 6½" Fabric E square as shown. Press.

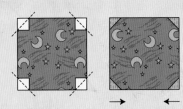

Fabric A = 1½ x 1½
Fabric E = 6½ x 6½

14. Sew unit from step 12 between one 1½" x 6½" Fabric A piece and unit from step 12 as shown. Press and label Unit 4.

Unit 4

6½

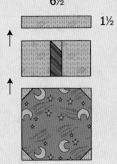 1½

15. Referring to photo on page 65, sew Units 2, 3, and 4 together. Press seams toward center.

16. Sew one 5½" x 19½" Fabric A piece to unit from step 15 as shown. Press.

19½

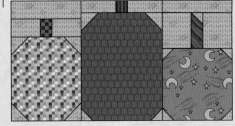 5½

Scarecrow TACTICS

Head: Fold 24" x 32" piece of muslin in half crosswise and sew top and side seams. Measure 6" from each top corner in both directions and mark. On one corner, bring marks together, gather, and tie off with a rubber band or string. Repeat for other corner. This forms a more rounded head. Turn right side out and stuff with polyester fiberfill. Cut triangle fabric pieces for eyes and nose. Glue triangles and yarn for mouth to head.

Stand: Use a heavy umbrella stand to hold the scarecrow. Cut a 2" x 2" board to 65" and insert into umbrella stand. Board may need some sanding to fit tightly. Place head on board and secure with twine.

Arms: Use an old broom or tree twig for arms. We screwed a Two Hole Strap to our 2" x 2" board to hold the broom in place.

Use old clothes and hat to dress scarecrow.

17. Referring to photo on page 65, sew Unit 1 to unit from step 16. Press.

18. Sew unit from step 17 between two 1" x 27½" Accent Border. Press toward border. Sew this unit between two 1" x 16½" Accent Border. Press.

Adding the Borders

1. Arrange and sew together four 2½" squares, two 2½" x 3½" pieces, one 2½" x 4½" piece, and two 2½" x 5½" assorted Fabric G pieces as shown. Press. Sew this unit to top of quilt. Press seam toward Accent border.

2½   3½   5½   2½   3½   2½   4½   2½   5½

2½

Pieced Top Border

2. Arrange and sew together two 2½" squares, two 2½" x 3½" pieces, two 2½" x 4½" pieces, and two 2½" x 5½" assorted Fabric G pieces as shown. Press. Sew this unit to bottom of quilt. Press seam toward Accent border.

5½   2½   2½   5½   3½   4½   4½   3½

2½

Pieced Bottom Border

3. Arrange and sew together two 2½" squares, one 2½" x 3½" piece, two 2½" x 4½" pieces, and one 2½" x 5½" assorted Fabric G pieces as shown. Press. Sew this unit to left side of quilt. Press seam toward Accent border.

4½   2½   4½   5½   3½   2½

2½

Pieced Left Border

4. Arrange and sew together five 2½" squares, two 2½" x 3½" pieces, and one 2½" x 4½" piece assorted Fabric G pieces as shown. Press. Sew this unit to right of quilt. Press seam toward Accent border.

3½   2½   2½   3½   2½   2½   4½   2½

2½

Pieced Right Border

Adding the Appliqués

Refer to appliqué instructions on page 93. Our instructions are for Quick-Fuse Appliqué, but if you prefer hand qppliqué add ¼"-wide seam allowances.

1. Use patterns on page 68 to trace "PUMPKINS" and leaf patterns on paper side of fusible web. Use appropriate fabrics to prepare all appliqués for fusing.

2. Refer to photo on page 65 and fuse "PUMPKINS" to quilt top. Finish appliqué edges with machine satin stitch or other decorative stitching as desired.

3. Cut leaf out and press to another leaf fabric. Trim around leaf shape with pinking shears.

Layering and Finishing

1. Referring to Layering the Quilt on page 94, arrange and baste backing, batting, and top together. Hand or machine quilt as desired.

2. Refer to Binding the Quilt on page 94. Using 2¾"-wide Binding strips, bind quilt to finish.

Adding the Embellishments

1. Referring to photo on page 65, and couching on page 95, attach a small piece of yarn to quilt for pumpkin vine.

2. Referring to photo on page 65, take a small tuck in leaf and tack to quilt.

Pumpkins in a Row Wall Quilt

Patterns are reversed for use with Quick-Fuse Applique (page 93)

Tracing Line _____

Note: Place the slightly larger 'P' at the beginning of word.

Pumpkin Leaf Pattern
Make 1

Pumpkin
POWER

These cute pumpkins grow quickly in your sewing room and will make a great centerpiece or autumn décor.

1. Referring to partial patterns below, make elliptical shape patterns for each pumpkin. Cut five elliptical shapes for each pumpkin.

2. With right sides together and using ¼"-wide seams, sew two elliptical shapes together, starting about 1" from top. Continue adding elliptical shapes until all five have been sewn together. At this point, the bottom should be completely enclosed and just the top remains open. Turn right side out.

3. Through top opening, pour 3-4 cups of bean bag pellets into cavity. Stuff pumpkin with fiberfill to desired fullness.

4. Cut a 20" piece of brass wire and fold in the middle. Wrap wire ends around pencil to create curlicues, then insert folded end into pumpkin opening.

5. Fold 7" x 14" wool piece in half to make 7" x 7" square. Fold diagonally to create triangular shape. Starting at the diagonal fold, roll wool tightly to create a stem shape that's narrower at the top and wider at the bottom. Secure with pins then hand-stitch. Place stem in hole and hand stitch opening closed, securing stem and curlicues in place. If desired, bend stem and secure with stitches.

6. Using pattern on page 68, make leaves as desired. Hand-stitch in place.

Materials Needed

Small Pumpkin - ⅓ yard
Large Pumpkin - ⅓ yard
Stems - 7" x 14" Wool scraps
Leaves - Wool scraps
Heavy Brass Wire for Curlicues
Polyester Fiberfill
Bean Bag Pellets

Pumpkin Power Elliptical Shape
Trace four times aligning placement lines to make one Elliptical Shape.

Large Pumpkin Tracing Line _____
Small Pumpkin Tracing Line _____
Placement Line _____

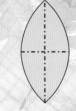

Welcome
BANNER

Getting Started

This quick and easy banner is just the thing to accent your door or lamppost.

Making the Banner

Using ¼"-wide seam allowance, sew 1½" x 12" Fabric B strip to 12" x 19½" Fabric A piece. Press.

Adding the Appliqués

Refer to appliqué instructions on page 92. Our instructions are for Quick-Fuse Appliqué, but if you prefer hand appliqué, reverse templates and add ¼"-wide seam allowance.

1. Use patterns on pages 54, 55, and 71 to trace one each of Large and Medium Pumpkins, Gourd, Corn, "WELCOME", and Banner Upper Arch on paper side of fusible web.

2. Refer to photo to position and fuse appliqués to quilt. Top of Upper Arch should meet top edge of Fabric A piece and side edges should match. Finish appliqué edges with blanket stitch or other decorative stitching as desired.

3. Trim away Background fabric from top of Upper Arch creating banner shape.

Layering and Finishing

1. Layer backing and quilt top, right sides together, on batting. Using ¼"-wide seam allowance, stitch sides and top edges leaving bottom edge free of stitching. Trim batting close to stitching and backing even with banner edges. Clip Upper Arch to seam line at inner corner, turn, and press.

2. Cut Timtex or mat board to banner shape and insert into banner opening. Press under ¼" on bottom edges and hand stitch opening closed. Quilt as desired.

3. Hand stitch hooks to back of banner. Cut chain to desired length, insert through hooks, and hang.

Greet family and guests at the door with a beautiful banner that proclaims a harvest welcome. The banner's arched top adds a feeling of tradition and antiquity.

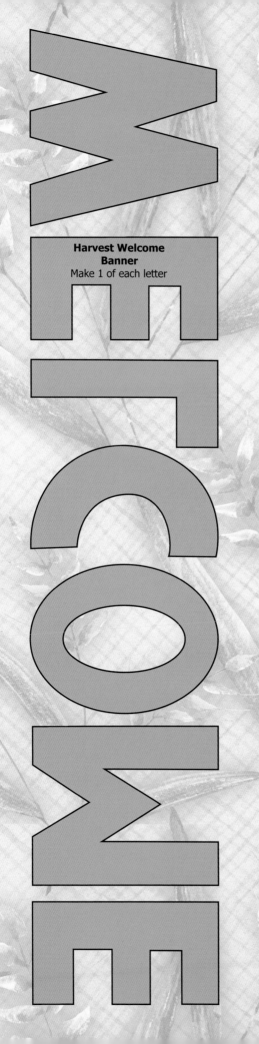

Harvest Welcome Banner
Make 1 of each letter

Materials Needed

Fabric A Background - ⅜ yard
    One 12" x 19½" piece

Fabric B Banner Accent - ⅙ yard
    One 1½" x 12" piece
    One 4½" x 12" piece

Backing - ½ yard
    One 14" x 22" piece

Batting - 14" x 22" piece

Appliqués - Assorted scraps

Lightweight Fusible Web - ⅜ yard

Timtex or Mat Board

Chain/Hooks

Harvest Welcome Banner
Patterns are reversed for use
with Quick-Fuse Applique (page 93)

Tracing Line _____
Placement Line _ _ _ _ _ _ _ _ _

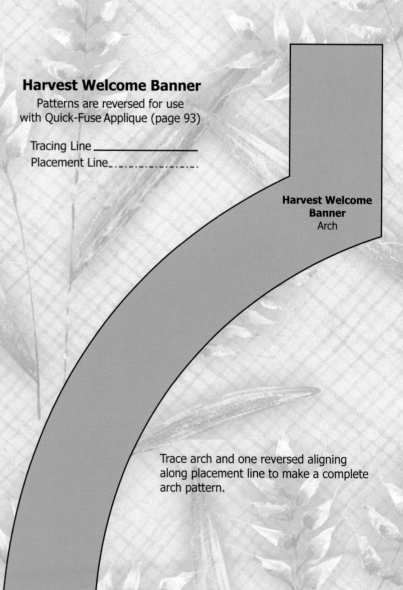

**Harvest Welcome
Banner**
Arch

Trace arch and one reversed aligning
along placement line to make a complete
arch pattern.

Holiday
TRADITIONS

Christmas MERRIMENT

Treasure your holiday traditions and create new memories with a joyful celebration of good food, heartwarming gifts, cozy quilts, and elegant decorations.

Log Cabin Christmas Lap Quilt

Christmas Bird Wall Quilt

Mosaic Ball

Christmas Bird Banners

Snowman Greeter Banner

Snowman Pillow

Birds 'n Flakes Ornaments

Snowflake Tree

Log Cabin Christmas
LAP QUILT

Log Cabin Christmas Lap Quilt Finished Size: 46" x 58"	FIRST CUT		SECOND CUT	
	Number of Strips or Pieces	Dimensions	Number of Pieces	Dimensions
LARGE LOG CABIN BLOCKS				
Fabric A Center ⅛ yard	1	3½" x 42"	8	3½" squares
Fabric B 1st Light ⅛ yard	2	1½" x 42"	8 8	1½" x 4½" 1½" x 3½"
Fabric C 1st Dark ¼ yard	3	1½" x 42"	8 8	1½" x 5½" 1½" x 4½"
Fabric D 2nd Light ¼ yard	3	2" x 42"	8 8	2" x 7" 2" x 5½"
Fabric E 2nd Dark ⅓ yard	4	2" x 42"	8 8	2" x 8½" 2" x 7"
Fabric F 3rd Light ½ yard	5	2½" x 42"	8 8	2½" x 10½" 2½" x 8½"
Fabric G 3rd Dark ½ yard	6	2½" x 42"	8 8	2½" x 12½" 2½" x 10½"
SMALL LOG CABIN BLOCKS				
Fabric A Center ⅛ yard each of 2 Fabrics	1*	2½" x 42" *cut for each fabric	8*	2½" squares
Fabric B 1st Light ⅛ yard each of 2 Fabrics	2*	1½" x 42" *cut for each fabric	8* 8*	1½" x 3½" 1½" x 2½"
Fabric C 1st Dark ⅛ yard each of 2 Fabrics	2*	1½" x 42" *cut for each fabric	8* 8*	1½" x 4½" 1½" x 3½"
Fabric D 2nd Light ¼ yard each of 2 Fabrics	3*	1½" x 42" *cut for each fabric	8* 8*	1½" x 5½" 1½" x 4½"
Fabric E 2nd Dark ¼ yard each of 2 Fabrics	3*	1½" x 42" *cut for each fabric	8* 8*	1½" x 6½" 1½" x 5½"
BORDERS				
First Border ⅓ yard	5	1½" x 42"	2	1½" x 36½"
Second Border ⅓ yard	5	2" x 42"	2	2" x 38½"
Outside Border ½ yard	5	2½" x 42"		
Binding ⅝ yard	6	2¾" x 42"		
Backing - 3 yards Batting - 52" x 64"				

Fabric Requirements and Cutting Instructions

Read all instructions before beginning and use ¼"-wide seam allowances throughout. Read Cutting Strips and Pieces on page 92 prior to cutting fabric.

Getting Started

The rich colors of the holiday season are featured in this quilt making it a great accent to your holiday décor. Large Log Cabin Blocks measure 12½" square (unfinished) and Small Log Cabin Blocks measure 6½" square (unfinished). Refer to Accurate Seam Allowance on page 92. Whenever possible use Assembly Line Method on page 92. Press seams in direction of arrows.

Making the Large Log Cabin Blocks

1. Sew one 3½" Fabric A square to one 1½" x 3½" Fabric B piece as shown. Press. Sew this unit to one 1½" x 4½" Fabric B piece. Press. Make eight.

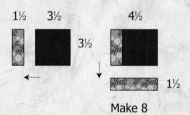

Make 8

2. Sew one unit from step 1 to one 1½" x 4½" Fabric C piece as shown. Press. Sew this unit to one 1½" x 5½" Fabric C piece. Press. Make eight.

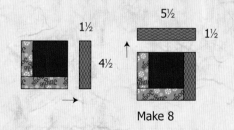

Make 8

The richness and warmth of holiday colors combine with the legacy of log cabin blocks to create a Christmas quilt that's sure to become an important part of your annual celebration. Two sizes of Log Cabin blocks create a pleasing variation to tradition.

3. Sew one unit from step 2 to one 2" x 5½" Fabric D piece as shown. Press. Sew this unit to one 2" x 7" Fabric D piece. Press. Make eight.

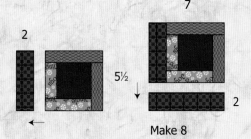

Make 8

4. Sew one unit from step 3 to one 2" x 7" Fabric E piece as shown. Press. Sew this unit to one 2" x 8½" Fabric E piece. Press. Make eight.

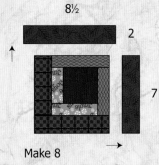

Make 8

5. Sew one unit from step 4 to one 2½" x 8½" Fabric F piece as shown. Press. Sew this unit to one 2½" x 10½" Fabric F piece. Press. Make eight.

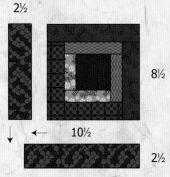

Make 8

6. Sew one unit from step 5 to one 2½" x 10½" Fabric G piece as shown. Press. Sew this unit to one 2½" x 12½" Fabric G piece. Press. Make eight. Block measures 12½" square.

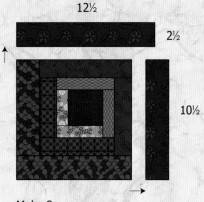

Make 8
Block measures 12½" square

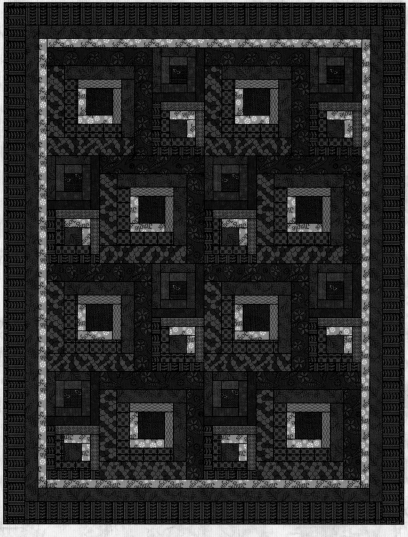

Log Cabin Christmas Lap Quilt
Finished Size: 46" x 58"

Making the Small Log Cabin Blocks

1. Sew one 2½" Fabric A square to one 1½" x 2½" Fabric B piece as shown. Press. Sew this unit to one 1½" x 3½" Fabric B piece. Press. Make eight.

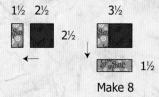

Make 8

2. Sew one unit from step 1 to one 1½" x 3½" Fabric C piece as shown. Press. Sew this unit to one 1½" x 4½" Fabric C piece. Press. Make eight.

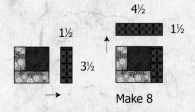

Make 8

3. Sew one unit from step 2 to one 1½" x 4½" Fabric D piece as shown. Press. Sew this unit to one 1½" x 5½" Fabric D piece. Press. Make eight.

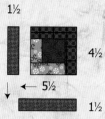

1½

4½

← 5½

1½

Make 8

4. Sew one unit from step 3 to one 1½" x 5½" Fabric E piece as shown. Press. Sew this unit to one 1½" x 6½" Fabric E piece. Press. Make eight.

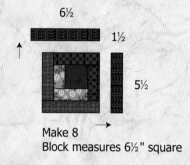

6½

1½

5½

Make 8
Block measures 6½" square

5. Repeat steps 1-4 to make eight small log cabin units in another color combination. Make eight.

Make 8
Block measures 6½" square

6. Sew one unit from step 5 to one unit from step 4. Press. Make eight Small Log Cabin Blocks. Block measures 6½" x 12½".

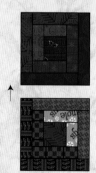

Make 8
Block measures 6½" x 12½"

Quilt Assembly

1. Referring to layout on page 76, rows 1 and 3, sew two Large Log Cabin Blocks and two Small Log Cabin Blocks together. Press seams in one direction. Make two.

2. Referring to layout on page 76, rows 2 and 4, sew two Small Log Cabin Blocks and two Large Cabin Blocks together. Press seams in opposite direction from step 1. Make two.

3. Referring to layout on page 76, arrange and sew rows from steps 1 and 2 together, alternately rows. Press.

Adding the Borders

1. Sew quilt between two 1½" x 36½" First Border Strips. Press seams toward border. Refer to Adding the Borders on page 94. Sew 1½" x 42" First Border strips together end-to-end to make one continuous 1½"-wide First Border strip. Measure quilt through center from top to bottom including borders just added. Cut two 1½"-wide First Border strips to this measurement. Sew to sides of quilt. Press.

2. Refer to step 1 to sew 2" x 38½" Second Border Strips to top and bottom of quilt. Press. Join, measure, and sew 2"-wide Second Border to sides. Press.

3. Refer to step 1 to join, measure, trim, and sew 2½"-wide Outside Border strips to top, bottom, and sides of quilt. Press.

Layering and Finishing

1. Cut backing crosswise into two equal pieces. Sew pieces together lengthwise to make one 54" x 80" (approximate) backing piece. Press and trim to 54" x 64".

2. Referring to Layering the Quilt on page 94, arrange and baste backing, batting, and top together. Hand or machine quilt as desired.

3. Refer to Binding the Quilt on page 94. Sew 2¾" x 42" binding strips end-to-end to make one continuous 2¾" binding strip. Bind quilt to finish.

Christmas Bird
WALL QUILT

Christmas Bird Wall Quilt Finished Size: 26" x 39½"	FIRST CUT		SECOND CUT	
	Number of Strips or Pieces	Dimensions	Number of Pieces	Dimensions
Fabric A Appliqué Background ½ yard each of 2 Fabrics	1*	12½" x 42" *cut for each fabric	2*	12½" squares
Fabric B Appliqué Block Accent ½ yard each of 2 Fabrics	2*	6½" x 42" *cut for each fabric	8*	6½" squares
Fabric C Log Cabin Center ⅛ yard	1	2½" x 42"	8	2½" squares
Fabric D Green Block Borders ⅙ yard each of 2 Fabrics	2*	1½" x 42" *cut for each fabric	4* 4* 4* 4*	1½" x 5½" 1½" x 4½" 1½" x 3½" 1½" x 2½"
Fabric E Red Block Borders ⅙ yard each of 2 Fabrics	2*	1½" x 42" *cut for each fabric	4* 4* 4* 4*	1½" x 6½" 1½" x 5½" 1½" x 4½" 1½" x 3½"
Fabric F Quilt Accent Border ⅛ yard	2	1¼" x 42"	2	1¼" x 24½"
Binding ⅝ yard**	4	4½" x 42" (1" finished binding)		

Backing - 1¼ yards
Batting - 30" x 43½"
Bird Appliqués - Assorted scraps
Lightweight Fusible Web - ½ yard

**Fabric must be 42"-wide or wider.

Fabric Requirements and Cutting Instructions

Read all instructions before beginning and use ¼"-wide seam allowances throughout. Read Cutting Strips and Pieces on page 92 prior to cutting fabric.

Getting Started

Observe these birds from the comfort of your own home during those long winter days by making this wall quilt. Each Bird Block measures 12½" square (unfinished) and the quilt is accented with 6½" square (unfinished) Log Cabin Blocks. Different placement of the same fabrics add interest to both the Log Cabin and Bird Blocks. Refer to Accurate Seam Allowance on page 92. Whenever possible use Assembly Line Method on page 92. Press seams in direction of arrows.

Making the Log Cabin Blocks

1. Sew one 2½" Fabric C square to one 1½" x 2½" Fabric D piece. Press toward Fabric D. Sew this unit to one 1½" x 3½" Fabric D piece as shown. Press. Make eight, four of each combination.

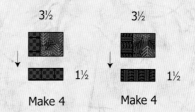

Make 4   Make 4

2. Sew one unit from step 1 to one 1½" x 3½" Fabric E piece as shown. Press. Sew this unit to one 1½" x 4½" Fabric E piece. Press. Make eight, four of each combination.

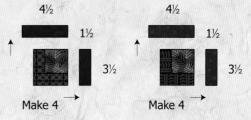

Make 4 →   Make 4 →

3. Sew one unit from step 2 to one 1½" x 4½" Fabric D piece as shown. Press. Sew this unit to one 1½" x 5½" Fabric D piece. Press. Make eight, four of each combination.

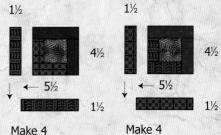

Make 4   Make 4

Four calling birds warble a holiday greeting on this naturally beautiful wall quilt. Log Cabin blocks accent four appliquéd birds combining tradition with an on-trend emphasis on nature. This lovely wall quilt will invite friends and family to stay a while and enjoy the splendor of the season.

4. Sew one unit from step 3 to one 1½" x 5½" Fabric E piece as shown. Press. Sew this unit to one 1½" x 6½" Fabric E piece. Press. Make eight, four of each combination. Block measures 6½" square.

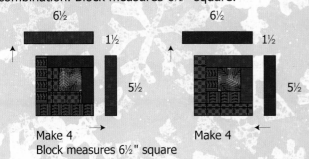

Make 4
Block measures 6½" square

Make 4

5. Arrange and sew four Log Cabin Blocks together, checking orientation of blocks prior to sewing. Press. Make 2.

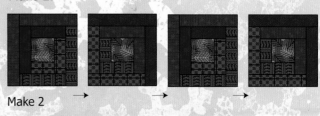

Make 2

Making the Bird Blocks

Refer to appliqué instructions on page 93. Our instructions are for Quick-Fuse Appliqué, but if you prefer hand appliqué, reverse templates and add ¼"-wide seam allowances.

1. Refer to Quick Corner Triangles on page 92. Making quick corner triangle units, sew four 6½" Fabric B squares to one 12½" Fabric A square. Press. Make four, two of each combination. Block measures 12½" square.

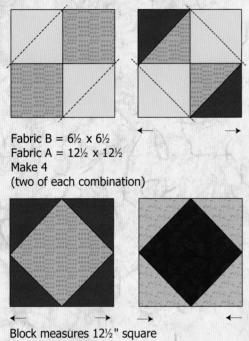

Fabric B = 6½ x 6½
Fabric A = 12½ x 12½
Make 4
(two of each combination)

Block measures 12½" square

2. Use patterns on page 81 to trace four of each bird, limb, leaves, and berries on paper side of fusible web. Refer to photo on page 79 and use appropriate fabrics to prepare all appliqués for fusing. Make two birds/branches of each color combination.

3. Refer to photo on page 79 to position and fuse appliqués to quilt blocks. Finish appliqué edges with machine satin stitch or other decorative stitching as desired.

Assembly

1. Refer to photo on page 79 to arrange all Bird Blocks so birds are positioned in the same direction and color combinations are opposing.

2. Sew two Bird Blocks, one of each combination together. Press. Make two.

3. Sew rows from step 2 together to make one unit. Press.

4. Sew unit from step 3 between two 1¼" x 24½" Fabric F strips. Press seams toward Fabric F.

5. Refer to photo on page 79 to sew unit from step 4 between two Log Cabin rows noting orientation of Log Cabin Block rows. Press seams toward Fabric F.

Layering and Finishing

1. Referring to Layering the Quilt on page 94, arrange and baste backing, batting, and top together. Hand or machine quilt as desired. Note: This quilt has a 1" finished binding. After quilting, trim batting and backing piece ¾" larger than quilt top outside edges.

2. Refer to Binding the Quilt on page 94. Using 4½"-wide binding strips, bind quilt to finish.

Mosaic BALL

This beautiful oversized ornament is perfect for indoor or outdoor decoration when combined with fresh greenery.

1. Glue mosaic pieces onto Styrofoam ball using Weldbond® in pattern desired and leaving about ⅛"-¼" between pieces. Work in sections and allow the adhesive to dry thoroughly after each application.

2. When ball is covered with glass and adhesive is completely dry, apply grout, wearing rubber gloves, and following manufacturer's directions for application, cleaning, and drying times.

Materials Needed

6" Styrofoam Ball

Glass Mosaic Pieces* – Variety of sizes and colors

Weldbond® Adhesive

Premixed Ceramic Tile Grout – Smooth White

Rubber Gloves, Bucket, Putty or Palette Knife, Grout Sponge

*Available at craft stores or internet.

Christmas Bird Wall Quilt

Tracing Line _____

Tracing Line . . . .

(will be hidden behind other fabrics)

Placement Line . . _ . . _ . . _ . . _ . . _ .

Christmas Bird
BANNERS

Materials Needed
for two banners

Background - ⅔ yard
   Two -22½" x 14½"

Top and Bottom Accents & Tabs - ½ yard

Backing - ¾ yard
   Two -24" x 16"

Flourish Appliqué - ½ yard

Bird - ⅛ yard

Branch, Leaves, Berries, and Bird Wing - Assorted scraps

Lightweight Fusible Web - 2 yards

Iron-on Interfacing - 1 yard

Beads for Eyes

Getting Started

This elegant banner set will add grace and beauty to your room. We used wool fabrics for its richness and texture, but banners can be made using other fabric combinations.

Adding the Appliqués

Refer to appliqué instructions on page 93. Our instructions are for Quick-Fuse Appliqué, but if you prefer hand appliqué, reverse templates and add ¼"-wide seam allowances if using cotton fabrics.

1. Follow instructions on pages 84 and 85 to enlarge patterns by 200% to make full size patterns, noting direction of pieces and quantity needed for each. Trace patterns on paper side of fusible web. Use appropriate fabrics to prepare all appliqués for fusing. Note: Extend bottom curve piece as instructed on page 84 to make whole pattern.

2. Following manufacturer's instructions fuse 22½" x 14½" piece of interfacing to back of Background piece.

3. Refer to photo on page 83 to position and fuse top and bottom curved accent pieces to 22½" x 14½" Background fabric. Refer to diagram below to mark center and 3" from each bottom corner. Draw a line connecting marks to make a pointed end. Cut on drawn line.

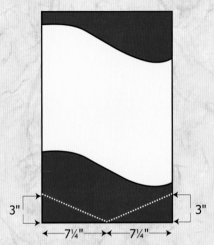

3"   3"

7¼"   7¼"

4. Refer to photo on page 83 to position and fuse appliqués to unit from step 3. Finish appliqué edges with hand or machine blanket stitch or use other decorative stitching as desired. Refer to photo to add bead for eye.

5. Center unit from step 4 on 24" x 16" backing piece. Finish unit edge with hand or machine blanket stitch or use other decorative stitching as desired. Trim backing piece ¼" away from banner unit edges.

6. Cut three 2" x 6" Tabs, fold each in half and position 2" x 3" folded tab on Banner back. Sew in place.

7. Repeat steps 1-6 to make second banner noting the direction of Top and Bottom Accent pieces and using other appliqué pattern pieces.

All the elegance, beneficence, and splendor of the holiday season are represented in these two beautiful banners. Graceful curves of red flow from one banner to the other while flourishes of bright green create a backdrop for the beautiful appliquéd birds.

Banner Bottom Pattern Piece

Paper-side of fusible web

Pattern underneath

3" 3"

For bottom curved-pattern pieces only trace enlarged pattern curve edge and extend side and bottom edges by 3" as shown above to make a complete pattern piece.

Enlarge pattern then extend pattern 3" as noted above.

Christmas Bird Banners

Enlarge 200% to complete banner project.

Pattern is reversed for use
with Quick-Fuse Appliqué (page 93)

Tracing Line _____

Tracing Line - - - - - - - - - - - - - - - - -
(will be hidden behind other fabrics)

*Permission to photocopy pages 84 and 85 is
granted by Debbie Mumm Inc. to successfully
complete Christmas Bird Banners.*

Enlarge pattern then extend pattern 3" as noted above.

Snowman Greeter
BANNER

Getting Started

Use assorted fabric textures such as cotton, fleece and cotton flannel to make this whimsical Snowman Banner. Refer to Accurate Seam Allowance on page 92. Whenever possible use Assembly Line Method on page 92. Press seams in direction of arrows.

Making the Log Cabin Blocks

1. Sew one 2½" Fabric B square to one 1½" x 2½" Fabric C piece. Press. Sew this unit to one 1½" x 3½" Fabric C piece as shown. Press. Make six.

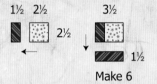

Make 6

2. Repeat step 1 to sew 1½" x 3½" and 1½" x 4½" Fabric D pieces, 1½" x 4½" and 1½" x 5½" Fabric E pieces, and 1½" x 5½" and 1½" x 6½" Fabric F pieces to unit from step 1. Press. Note: Last seam may need to be re-pressed when sewing blocks together. Make six. Block measures 6½" square.

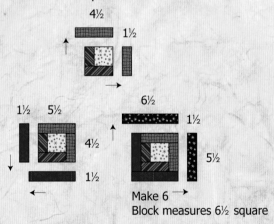

Make 6
Block measures 6½ square

3. Refer to photo on page 87 to arrange and sew three Log Cabin Blocks together to make a row. Press. Make two.

4. Sew one 18½" x 30½" Fabric A piece between two Log Cabin rows, checking orientation of rows prior to sewing. Press.

Snowman Greeter Banner Finished Size: 19½" x 43½"	FIRST CUT	
	Number of Strips or Pieces	Dimensions
Fabric A Background ⅝ yard	1	18½" x 30½"
Fabric B Log Cabin Blocks ⅛ yard	6	2½" squares
Fabric C Log Cabin Blocks ⅛ yard	6	1½" x 3½"
	6	1½" x 2½"
Fabric D Log Cabin Blocks ⅙ yard	6	1½" x 4½"
	6	1½" x 3½"
Fabric E Log Cabin Blocks ⅙ yard	6	1½" x 5½"
	6	1½" x 4½"
Fabric F Log Cabin Blocks ⅙ yard	6	1½" x 6½"
	6	1½" x 5½"
Binding ½ yard	4	3½" x 42" (¾" finished binding)

Backing - 1⅓ yard
Batting - 23" x 47"
Scarf - ⅙ yard
    One 4½" x 42"
Snowman Body Appliqué - ⅜ yard
Appliqués - Assorted scraps
Assorted Buttons - Black, Red and White
Lightweight Fusible Web - 1 yard

Fabric Requirements and Cutting Instructions

Read all instructions before beginning and use ¼"-wide seam allowances throughout. Read Cutting Strips and Pieces on page 92 prior to cutting fabric.

Adding the Appliqués

Refer to appliqué instructions on page 93. Our instructions are for Quick-Fuse Appliqué, but if you prefer hand appliqué, reverse templates and add ¼"-wide seam allowances.

1. Use patterns on page 88 to trace Snowman's hat, nose, two arms, bird, two holly leaves, one large snowflake, two medium snowflakes, and six small snowflakes on paper side of fusible web. Use appropriate fabrics to prepare all appliqués for fusing.

2. Use patterns on page 95 to trace circles, one 7", one 9¼" and one 11½", on paper side of fusible web. Use appropriate fabrics to prepare all appliqués for fusing.

3. Refer to photo to position and fuse appliqués to quilt. Finish appliqué edges with machine satin stitch or other decorative stitching as desired. Note: Large and medium snowflakes are fused to background piece and small snowflakes are fused to the center of each Log Cabin block.

4. Fold 4½" x 42" Scarf strip lengthwise right sides together and sew all edges using ¼"-wide seam allowance. Cut scarf in half to make two equal pieces. Clip corners, turn right side out and press.

5. Refer to photo for scarf placement. Adjust scarf to desired length and trim raw edge as needed. Fold scarf raw edge under ¼" and stitch to outside edge of top snowman body piece. Repeat for other side. Tie scarf and tack in place.

6. Referring to Layering the Quilt on page 94, arrange and baste backing, batting, and top together. Hand or machine quilt as desired. Note: This quilt has a ¾" finished binding. After quilting, trim batting and backing piece ½" larger than quilt top outside edge.

7. Refer to Binding the Quilt on page 94. Use 3½"-wide binding strips, bind quilt to finish.

8. Embellish with buttons as desired. Note: Our snowman uses two different size black buttons for snowman's face, three different red buttons for holly berries, and two different size buttons stacked and sewn to center of each medium and large snowflake.

Friends and family will be enchanted by this happy fellow as he tips his hat to greet new arrivals. Flannel and berber combine for an extra-cozy attitude on this unusually shaped wall quilt.

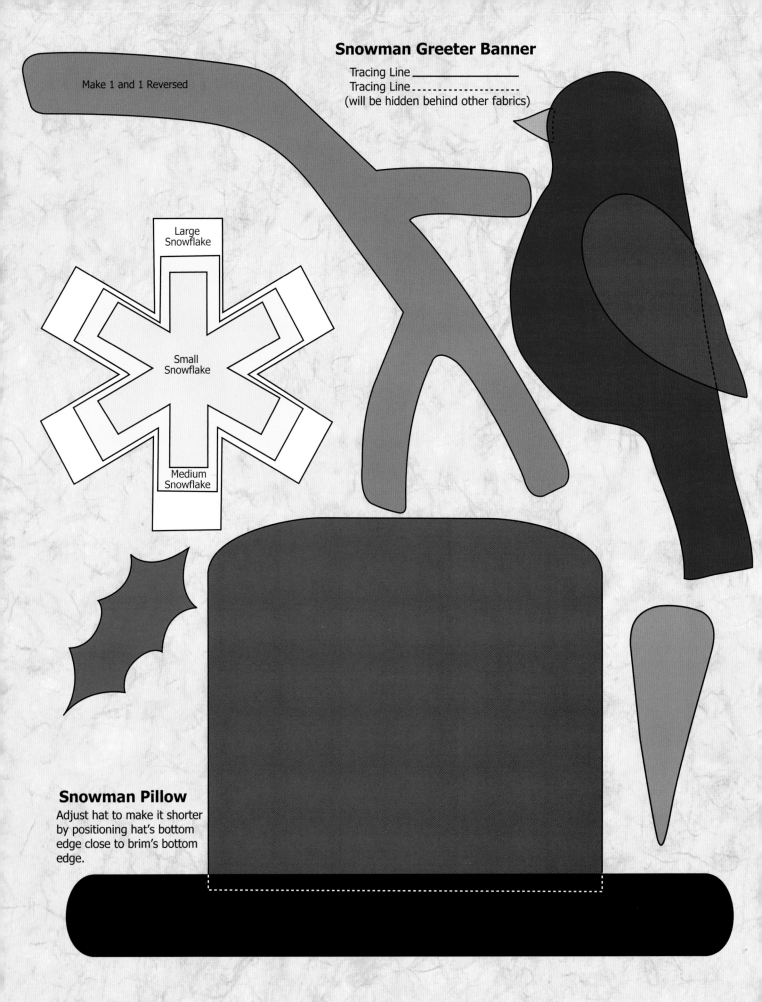

Make 1 and 1 Reversed

Snowman Greeter Banner

Tracing Line _____
Tracing Line - - - - - - - - - - - - - - - - - - -
(will be hidden behind other fabrics)

Large
Snowflake

Small
Snowflake

Medium
Snowflake

Snowman Pillow

Adjust hat to make it shorter
by positioning hat's bottom
edge close to brim's bottom
edge.

Snowman PILLOW

This happy snowman pillow will add whimsy and color to your holiday décor. Make one for a gift to bring a smile to a friend's face.

Materials Needed

Fabric A (Background) - ½ yard
    One - 14½" square
Fabric B (Corners) - ⅓ yard
    Four - 7½" squares
Border - ⅙ yard
    Two - 1½" x 16½"
    Two - 1½" x 14½"
Backing - ½ yard
    Two - 11" x 16½"
Lining and Batting - 20" x 20"
Snowman Appliqués - Assorted scraps
Bow Tie - Scrap
    One - 4½" x 5½"
Assorted Buttons - Black and Red
Lightweight Fusible Web - ¼ yard
16" Pillow Form

Making the Pillow

1. Refer to Quick Corner Triangles on page 92. Making quick corner triangle units, sew four 7½" Fabric B squares to one 14½" Fabric A square as shown. Press.

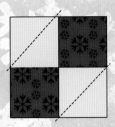 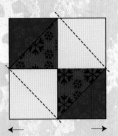

Fabric B = 7½" x 7½"
Fabric A = 14½" x 14½"

2. Sew unit from step 1 between two 1½" x 14½" Border strips. Press. Sew this unit between two 1½" x 16½" Border strips. Press.

3. Refer to appliqué instructions on page 93. Use patterns on page 88 to trace Snowman hat, nose and two holly leaves on paper side of fusible web. Use pattern on page 95 to draw one 5½" circle on the paper side of fusible web. Use appropriate fabrics to prepare all appliqués for fusing. Note: See Snowman Pillow hat instructions on page 88.

4. Refer to photo to position and fuse appliqués to pillow top. Finish appliqué edges with machine satin stitch or other decorative stitching as desired.

5. Refer to Finishing Pillows on page 94, step 1, to prepare pillow top for quilting. Quilt as desired.

6. Sew buttons in place for Snowman eyes, mouth, and holly berries.

7. Fold 4½" x 5½" Bowtie piece lengthwise right sides together. Using ¼"-wide seam allowance, stitch leaving a 3" opening for turning. Turn right side out, press and hand stitch opening closed. Gather center of tie and secure. Refer to photo to arrange tie on pillow and tack in place.

8. Use two 11" x 16½" backing pieces and refer to Finishing Pillows, page 94, steps 2-4, to sew backing. Insert 16" pillow form or refer to Pillow Forms page 95 and use two 16½" square pieces of fabric and fiberfill to make a pillow form if desired.

Birds 'n Flakes ORNAMENTS

Tiny birds on branches or simple
snowflakes make enticing ornaments
for your nature-inspired tree.

Getting Started

These ornaments are so quick and easy to make you'll
want to make extra to add to your Christmas packages.
Instructions are for Quick-Fuse but if you prefer, use fabric
glue. Refer to page 95 for 3½" and 3" circle patterns.

Making the Bird Ornament

Use Bird Ornament pattern below. Trace bird, branch, two
leaves, and one 3" circle on paper side of fusible web.
Trace a 3½" circle on wool scrap. Use appropriate fabrics to
prepare all appliqués for fusing. Use pinking shears to cut
out circles on drawn lines. Center and fuse one 3" and one
3½" circle together. Refer to photo to position and fuse bird,
branch and leaves on circle unit. Note: Some appliqué edges
extend beyond 3½" circle edge. Add ribbon for hanger as
desired. Add bead for eye and berry accents if desired.

Making the Snowflake Ornament

Using Snowflake pattern on page 88, trace one medium
snowflake and one 3" circle on paper side of fusible web. For
added stability, fuse circle to another piece of wool scrap.
Use pinking shears to cut out circle on drawn line. Fold a 4"
ribbon in half for hanger. Fuse snowflake to circle placing
hanger ends between one snowflake spoke and background
circle. Glue additional trims to snowflake as desired.

Materials Needed

Appliqué - Assorted wool scraps
Trims - Assorted scraps
Pinking Shears
Fabric Glue
Heavyweight Fusible Web
Beads (Optional)

Bird Ornament
Pattern is reversed for use
with Quick-Fuse Applique (page 93)

Tracing Line _____
Tracing Line - - - - - - - - - - - - - - - - - -
(will be hidden behind other fabrics)

Snowflake
TREE

Snowflakes and buttons decorate a wooly green tree on this terrific table topper. Older children will love making this tree as a gift or to decorate a sideboard or table.

Making the Tree

1. Using mat, ruler, and rotary cutter with pinking blade cut ¾"-wide strips from green wool. Six to ten strips are needed depending on how tightly wool is wrapped around tree form. Using straight pins to hold strips at beginning and end, wrap wool around the tree form, starting at the bottom and overlapping top edge.

2. Wrap silver ribbon around tree securing with pins.

3. Using patterns on page 88, make two small, one medium, and one large snowflake from white wool or felt. Make two small and one large snowflake from red wool or felt. Referring to photo, position and use white pins to hold snowflakes on the tree.

4. Referring to photo, position red and white buttons on tree and use pins to hold until you are happy with placement. Glue buttons to tree using tacky glue; hold with pins until glue dries.

5. To make tree topper, iron fusible web to a 3" x 3" piece of red wool or felt. Trace medium snowflake on felt piece. Using a matching piece of wool or felt, iron pieces together, embedding about three-quarters of a toothpick between the pieces of wool at a snowflake point. Cut out snowflake through both layers. Decorate snowflake with white glass head pins. Put a dab of glue on each pin head and stick through snowflake point. When glue is dry, use a wire cutter to cut off pin shank on back side of topper. Insert topper into top of tree using the toothpick.

6. Paint small flowerpot with brown acrylic paint. Two or more coats may be needed for good coverage. Turn flowerpot upside down and glue to bottom of foam tree to serve as a trunk.

Materials Needed

16" Green Styrofoam Tree Form
Fat Quarter Green Wool
Red and White Felted Wool*
   or Felt – Scraps
Red and White Buttons – Assorted sizes
Rotary Cutter with Pinking Blade
Cutting Mat and Ruler
¼" Silver Ribbon – 2 yards
1⅜" White Glass Head Straight Pins
Clear-Drying Craft Glue
Heavyweight Fusible Web – Scrap
Toothpick
Small Flowerpot
Brown Craft Paint

*See directions on page 95.

General DIRECTIONS

Cutting Strips and Pieces

We recommend washing cotton fabrics in cold water and pressing before making projects in this book. Using a rotary cutter, see-through ruler, and a cutting mat, cut the strips and pieces for the project. If indicated on the Cutting Chart, some will need to be cut again into smaller strips and pieces. Make second cuts in order shown to maximize use of fabric. The yardage amounts and cutting instructions are based on an approximate fabric width of 42".

Pressing

Pressing is very important for accurate seam allowances. Press seams using either steam or dry heat with an "up and down" motion. Do not use side-to-side motion as this will distort the unit or block. Set the seam by pressing along the line of stitching, then press seams to one side as indicated by project instructions and diagram arrows.

Twisting Seams

When a block has several seams meeting in the center as shown, there will be less bulk if seam allowances are pressed in a circular type direction and the center intersection "twisted". Remove 1-2 stitches in the seam allowance to enable the center to twist and lay flat. This technique aids in quilt assembly by allowing the seams to fall opposite each other when repeated blocks are next to each other. The technique works well with 4-patch blocks, pinwheel blocks, and quarter-square triangle blocks.

Accurate Seam Allowance

Accurate seam allowances are always important, but especially when the blocks contain many pieces and the quilt top contains multiple pieced borders. If each seam is off as little as 1/16", you'll soon find yourself struggling with components that just won't fit.

To ensure seams are a perfect 1/4"-wide, try this simple test: Cut three strips of fabric, each exactly 1½" x 12". With right sides together, and long raw edges aligned, sew two strips together, carefully maintaining a 1/4" seam. Press seam to one side. Add the third strip to complete the strip set. Press and measure. The finished strip set should measure 3½" x 12". The center strip should measure 1"-wide, the two outside strips 1¼"-wide, and the seam allowances exactly 1/4".

If your measurements differ, check to make sure that seams have been pressed flat. If strip set still doesn't "measure up," try stitching a new strip set, adjusting the seam allowance until a perfect 1/4"-wide seam is achieved.

Assembly Line Method

Whenever possible, use an assembly line method. Position pieces right sides together and line up next to sewing machine. Stitch first unit together, then continue sewing others without breaking threads. When all units are sewn, clip threads to separate. Press seams in direction of arrows as shown in step-by-step project diagrams.

Quick Corner Triangles

Quick corner triangles are formed by simply sewing fabric squares to other squares or rectangles. The directions and diagrams with each project illustrate what size pieces to use and where to place squares on the corresponding piece. Follow steps 1–3 below to make quick corner triangle units.

1. With pencil and ruler, draw diagonal line on wrong side of fabric square that will form the triangle. This will be your sewing line.

   Sewing line

2. With right sides together, place square on corresponding piece. Matching raw edges, pin in place, and sew ON drawn line. Trim off excess fabric, leaving 1/4"-wide seam allowance as shown.

   Trim 1/4" away from sewing line

3. Press seam in direction of arrow as shown in step-by-step project diagram. Measure completed quick corner triangle unit to ensure the greatest accuracy.

   Finished quick corner triangle unit

Fussy Cut

To make a "fussy cut," carefully position ruler or template over a selected design in fabric. Include seam allowances before cutting desired pieces.

Quick-Fuse Appliqué

Quick-fuse appliqué is a method of adhering appliqué pieces to a background with fusible web. For quick and easy results, simply quick-fuse appliqué pieces in place. Use sewable, lightweight fusible web for the projects in this book unless otherwise indicated. Finish raw edges with stitching as desired. Laundering is not recommended unless edges are finished.

1. With paper side up, lay fusible web over appliqué pattern. Leaving ½" space between pieces, trace all elements of design. Cut around traced pieces, approximately ¼" outside traced line.

fusible web

2. With paper side up, position and press fusible web to wrong side of selected fabrics. Follow manufacturer's directions for iron temperature and fusing time. Cut out each piece on traced line.

fabric-wrong side

3. Remove paper backing from pieces. A thin film will remain on wrong side of fabric. Position and fuse all pieces of one appliqué design at a time onto background, referring to photos for placement. Fused design will be the reverse of traced pattern.

Appliqué Pressing Sheet

An appliqué pressing sheet is very helpful when there are many small elements to apply using a quick-fuse appliqué technique. The pressing sheet allows small items to be bonded together before applying them to the background. The sheet is coated with a special material that prevents fusible web from adhering permanently to the sheet. Follow manufacturer's directions. Remember to let fabric cool completely before lifting it from the appliqué sheet. If not cooled, the fusible web could remain on the sheet instead of on the fabric.

For accurate layout, place a line drawing of finished project under pressing sheet. Use this as a guide to adhere pieces.

Machine Appliqué

This technique should be used when you are planning to launder quick-fuse projects. Several different stitches can be used: small narrow zigzag stitch, satin stitch, blanket stitch, or another decorative machine stitch. Use an open toe appliqué foot if your machine has one. Use a stabilizer to obtain even stitches and help prevent puckering. Always practice first to check machine settings.

1. Fuse all pieces following Quick-Fuse Appliqué directions.

2. Cut a piece of stabilizer large enough to extend beyond the area to be stitched. Pin to the wrong side of fabric.

3. Select thread to match appliqué.

4. Following the order that appliqués were positioned, stitch along the edges of each section. Anchor beginning and ending stitches by tying off or stitching in place two or three times.

5. Complete all stitching, then remove stabilizer.

Hand Appliqué

Hand appliqué is easy when you start out with the right supplies. Cotton and machine embroidery thread are easy to work with. Pick a color that matches the appliqué fabric as closely as possible. Use appliqué or silk pins for holding shapes in place and a long, thin needle, such as a sharp, for stitching.

1. Make a template for every shape in the appliqué design. Use a dotted line to show where pieces overlap.

2. Place template on right side of appliqué fabric. Trace around template.

3. Cut out shapes ¼" beyond traced line.

4. Position shapes on background fabric, referring to quilt layout. Pin shapes in place.

5. When layering and stitching appliqué shapes, always work from background to foreground. Where shapes overlap, do not turn under and stitch edges of bottom pieces. Turn and stitch the edges of the piece on top.

6. Use the traced line as your turn-under guide. Entering from the wrong side of the appliqué shape, bring the needle up on the traced line. Using the tip of the needle, turn under the fabric along the traced line. Using blind stitch, stitch along folded edge to join the appliqué shape to the background fabric. Turn under and stitch about ¼" at a time.

Adding the Borders

1. Measure quilt through the center from side to side. Trim two border strips to this measurement. Sew to top and bottom of quilt. Press seams toward border.

2. Measure quilt through the center from top to bottom, including borders added in step 1. Trim border strips to this measurement. Sew to sides and press. Repeat to add additional borders.

Layering the Quilt

1. Cut backing and batting 4" to 8" larger than quilt top.

2. Lay pressed backing on bottom (right side down), batting in middle, and pressed quilt top (right side up) on top. Make sure everything is centered and that backing and batting are flat. Backing and batting will extend beyond quilt top.

3. Begin basting in center and work toward outside edges. Baste vertically and horizontally, forming a 3"–4" grid. Baste or pin completely around edge of quilt top. Quilt as desired. Remove basting.

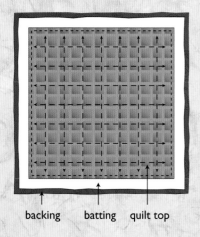

backing   batting   quilt top

Binding the Quilt

1. Trim batting and backing to ¼" beyond raw edge of quilt top. This will add fullness to binding.

2. Join binding strips to make one continuous strip if needed. To join, place 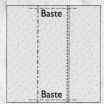 ←trim strips perpendicular to each other, right sides together, and draw a diagonal line. Sew on drawn line and trim triangle extensions, leaving a ¼"-wide seam allowance. Continue stitching ends together to make the desired length. Press seams open.

3. Fold and press binding strips in half lengthwise with wrong sides together.

4. Measure quilt through center from side to side. Cut two binding strips to this measurement. Lay binding strips on top and bottom edges of quilt top with raw edges of binding and quilt top aligned. Sew through all layers, ¼" from quilt edge. Press binding away from quilt top.

Front of Quilt

5. Measure quilt through center from top to bottom, including binding just added. Cut two binding strips to this measurement and sew to sides through all layers, including binding just added. Press.

6. Folding top and bottom first, fold binding around to back then repeat with sides. Press and pin in position. Hand-stitch binding in place using a blind stitch.

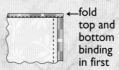 ←fold top and bottom binding in first

Finishing Pillows

1. Layer batting between pillow top and lining. Baste. Hand or machine quilt as desired. Trim batting and lining even with raw edge of pillow top.

2. Narrow hem one long edge of each backing piece by folding under ¼" to wrong side. Press. Fold under ¼" again to wrong side. Press. Stitch along folded edge.

3. With sides up, lay one backing piece over second piece so hemmed edges overlap, making backing unit the same measurement as the pillow top. Baste backing pieces together at top and bottom where they overlap.

4. With right sides together, position and pin pillow top to backing. Using ¼"-wide seam, sew around edges, trim corners, turn right side out, and press.

Embroidery Stitch Guide

French Knot   Running Stitch

Blanket Stitch

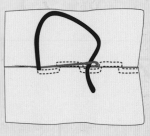

Blind Stitch